Shapiro Turns Racist.
– Geenstijl.nl

You should have more pizza on your shirt. – Dick Maas

Hey! That's my bike!
– Dutch guy

I think you were looking for Jesus.
– Chuck Woolery

I hope this kid doesn't come to me to extend his residence permit. – Fred Teeven

Stop. Talking.
– Seth Meyers

Do you stand by anything you say?
Or do you just sell yourself out when it's convenient?
– Hans Teeuwen

Shapiro, it's simple. Follow our traditions or get out.' – online comment #37

HOW TO BE ORANGE

An Alternative Dutch Assimilation Course

By Gregory Scott Shapiro

Illustrated by Floor de Goede
With a foreword by William of Orange

FOREWORD

I'm William of Orange. You may know me as 'William the Silent.' But I cannot keep silent about this book. Yes, I was silent for a while about the atrocities of the Spanish Inquisition, but that's because I've always honored the King of Spain. That brings me to How to Be Orange lesson 1: Keep Spain happy. They will no doubt be the economic superpower for centuries to come.

You may also know me as 'William of Orange.' Which is why Mr. Shapiro has asked me to write this foreword. It's not easy being Orange. Every time I say I'm proud to be from the United Provinces, there's always someone reminding me I'm not really from here. They call me names, saying I'm actually from Nassau in Germany – or Orange in France. Now that I'm in charge, I'll make sure we forever eliminate the word *allochtoon*. That brings me to How to Be Orange lesson 2: Be proud of being *allochtoon*. Some of the most famous Dutch thinkers are.

If there's one thing I hope you take away from this book, it's this: long live the Republic! I gave everything I had to throw off the monarchy and to blaze a trail for a new system of government, based on self-rule. May we always have the right to self-determination, such as the right to elect our city Mayors. That brings me to How to Be Orange lesson number 3: You have a right to your own opinion. In fact, to be Orange, you MUST PROMISE TO DISAGREE. With everyone. Even yourself.

And if anyone told me this country would become a monarchy, I'd pull off my own *moustache* in rage. Or – at least if we ever do have a monarchy – I hope they'll have the good sense to avoid inbreeding and get some foreign blood into the mix.

William of Orange, Delft 1584

Published by XPat Media, Van Boetzelaerlaan 153, 2581 AR, The Hague, the Netherlands
Tel.: +31(0)70 306 33 10 / +31(0)10 427 10 22 – E-mail: info@xpat.nl

COVER ILLUSTRATION AND DESIGN Floor de Goede
COVER PHOTO Adrie Mouthaan
INTERIOR DESIGN Bram Vandenberge
CARTOONS Floor de Goede
PHOTOGRAPHS The author
FINAL EDITING Stephanie Dijkstra
PRINTING DZS grafik
DISTRIBUTION www.scriptum.nl

ISBN 978 90 5594 800 0 | NUR 370

www.xpat.nl
www.howtobeorange.nl
www.gregshapiro.nl

This book is a work of non-fiction, based on the life, experiences and recollections of the author. The author reserves the right to adapt or streamline details for the sake of privacy or expediency. Quotes, events and details are not a reliable source of journalistic accuracy; rather, they are subjective tools used to tell a story. The author has stated to the publisher that, while certain details may have been changed, the essential details are based on true experience. Portions of the text have appeared in stage shows at Boom Chicago Comedy Theater, as blog pieces on Dutchnews.nl, and in The XPat Journal. The author extends his gratitude for the help he received in developing the material.

THE AUTHOR

Gregory Shapiro – the American Netherlander – moved to the Netherlands in 1994. After ten years he completed the equivalent of a Dutch Assimilation Course and received a Dutch passport. By now he can write in Dutch, but it still reads like a bad version of Google Translate. Shapiro married a Dutch woman and writes about Dutch culture at her insistence. Shapiro lives in Amsterdam with his wife and their two children and talks about himself in the third person.

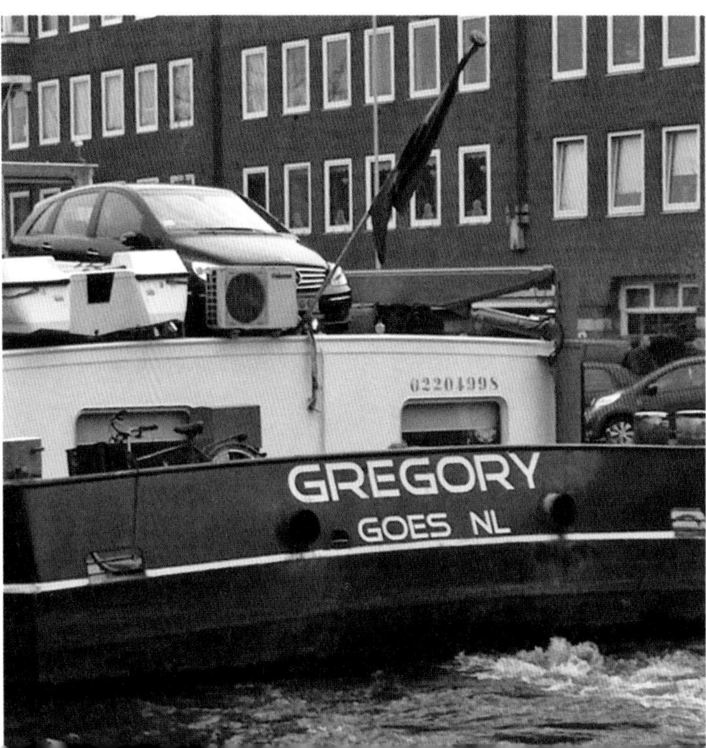

CONTENTS

Foreword 4
Introduction 10
Prologue 13

PART 1

1 Dutch Identity: Who Are We? 15
2 Dunglish 20
3 Dutch Culture for Dummies 30
4 Culture Shock Therapy 38
5 My Multi-Culti Nightmare 46
6 Waste Not 58
7 It's the Little Differences 66
8 How the Dutch See Themselves 71
9 Politician of the Year 79
10 Pain Tolerance 89
11 Sint's Little Helper 100
12 Acting Dutch 111
13 Dutch Meetings are from Mars 121
14 Dutch Honesty + Dutch Courage 128
15 No Subsidy for You 135
16 The Open Street is Closed 144
17 Overcrowding, Overpaying 153
18 Dutch Housing and Full Frontal Nudity 158
19 The Real Henk & Ingrid 173

20 Dutch Education: Race to the Middle! 186
21 'Benefit Tourism,' Meet 'Brain Drain' 191
22 Dutch Service – an Oxymoron? 197
23 Ranking the Standards 208
24 Dutch Identity: A New Ombudsman 215

PART 2

How to Be Orange: The Assimilation Exam 218

Epilogue 239
Acknowledgments 240

INTRODUCTION

This book is inspired by the stage show 'How to Be Orange: Making the Dutch Take Their Own Assimilation Course.' If you're looking for an official guide to Dutch culture, this is not it. If you're looking for one man's completely subjective and utterly biased impression of Dutch culture, then you've come to the right place.

Some people have split personalities. I have split nationalities. It's what I call 'MND:' Multiple Nationality Disorder.

I happen to live in Amsterdam, and a lot of this book takes place there. But MND can happen anywhere, from Maastricht to Den Haag to Enschede to Groningen. If you've ever lived outside the country where you grew up – as many Dutch have – then you could be living with MND.

See if any of these MND symptoms sounds familiar.

✔ I grew up in America with a dessert called 'Dutch Apple Pie.' The recipe involved sticky, grey, apple-flavored goo, filled with glucose and presented in a soggy crust. When I came to the Netherlands and ordered apple pie, I tasted real chunks of apple and a real butter crust. Enlightened, I took the recipe back to the US. Proudly, I presented it to my friends and family, and they were disappointed: 'This is not the real Dutch apple pie, is it?'

- ✔ I went back to my hometown and got culture shock. I'd been living abroad for over a year, and suddenly these people I'd grown up with looked foreign. Had they all changed since I'd been away? In particular, everyone's eyeglasses looked huge. Had America developed some new trend while I'd been gone? … And then I realized: nothing in America had changed. The only thing that had changed was my perception of what standard eyewear should look like, based on the tiny little reading glasses that Dutch people call 'normal.' When it comes to eyewear, Dutch people seem to think: 'It's such a tiny country, we wouldn't want to see too much of it at any one time.'

- ✔ I went back to the States and met some friends at a bar. They started teasing me for dressing like a 'Euro-fag.' Why? Because I was wearing 'skinny jeans' – aka clothes that actually fit my body. I looked around, and they were all wearing matching outfits: loose-fit shirts and loose-fit trousers, combined with active outerwear from Columbia, Patagonia or North Face – because you never know when you might need to climb a mountain in Chicago.

When you no longer feel completely at home anywhere, that's MND. This book is for you.

FOR INEZ

PROLOGUE

Amsterdam Day One

The date was April 4, 1994. The question was, 'Would I be willing to give up my acting career in Manhattan to come do comedy with my old friends, who'd set up a theater called Boom Chicago - in Amsterdam?' It sounded like a crazy idea. But - since I was living on tips and paying rent via credit card - the answer was an immediate YES.

My idea of Amsterdam was the one shared by most Americans, I suppose: The Golden Age, Anne Frank, then sex & drugs and downhill from there. To be honest, what I'd expected was one big red light district, full of grand, old buildings that had been left to crumble. I was in for a lovely surprise.

I remember getting off the plane at Schiphol Airport and thinking there must have been a mistake. It was such a modern, sleek, well-designed airport that I thought, 'this can't be Amsterdam.' It seemed more like a model for a modern American airport. In fact, that's exactly what it was. Shortly afterward, the Dutch would be called upon to redesign part of JFK, including the now iconic black-on-yellow information signs. And I'm going to sound like a travel writer, but I was pleasantly surprised at Amsterdam's baggage carts. They were actually larger – LARGER! – than their American counterparts. And they were free of charge. I had seriously misjudged the Netherlands.

The signs were in English. The ads were for Heineken. And the first thing I saw out of Customs was a Burger King. I thought I was in Pittsburgh.

And the charm offensive continued. Instead of having to surrender my baggage cart, I was able to take it right down to the train platform. It was my first time on a walkway escalator, and the handbrake on my baggage cart actually worked. Within one hour, I'd already started to redefine my definition of 'Second World Country.' That term was now reserved for JFK International.

CHAPTER 1

Dutch Identity: Who Are We?

Is there one Dutch identity? I haven't found it... Nederland is too diverse to sum up in any one cliché. – Máxima Zorreguieta, House of Orange

MÁXIMA SAYS DUTCH IDENTITY DOESN'T EXIST. – Dutch media

What am I doing here? Not long after Máxima's infamous quote, I was invited to a seminar on Dutch culture entitled 'Dutch Identity: Who Are We?' I was to take part in a panel discussion and share my experiences, along with other internationals. I said *yes*. But I didn't know what I was getting into.

The seminar started with a panel of elder Dutchmen: experts on Dutch culture, captains of Dutch industry, and some members of the government. The majority agreed that Máxima was wrong. There IS a Dutch identity. But they couldn't agree on what it was, exactly. I remember thinking to myself, 'If you guys can't figure out the Dutch identity, who will?'

Perhaps it's no wonder that the panel couldn't agree. According to the seminar's first speaker, part of the Dutch identity is the need to disagree. Ever since they threw off Spanish Catholicism, the Dutch have celebrated their right to their own opinion, even if that means debating everything. In my experience, this is pretty true. When I introduced my mother to my Dutch family for the first time, and someone told her 'nice outfit,' it was my Dutch father-in-law who said 'I don't think so.' And we got to hear a lengthy monologue on everything wrong with American fashion. For a tolerant people, the Dutch can be very judgmental.

The speaker summed it up with an ironic twist. Historically, the Dutch are very independent-minded. But they're also non-hierarchical. No one wants to be on top. Therefore, he said, Nederland is the least chauvinistic country in Europe. The speaker explained it like this: 'We Dutch are rather proud of our accomplishments, our culture, and our contributions to world society. But we are deathly allergic to taking any credit for it.' In essence – if the Dutch do have a national identity – they don't feel comfortable acknowledging it.

Up next was the panel. I was invited to sit onstage with a Chinese law student, a Turkish telecom entrepreneur, a Polish consultant, and a Dutchman, who was former head of international investment for Rabobank. What started off as a panel quickly turned into an impassioned monologue by Mr. Rabobank. He agreed that the Dutch are non-hierarchical by nature, and – in his experience – that's why they are a nation of followers. 'We don't need a seminar on management; we need a seminar on leadership! We have enough managers – look at the Dutch Cabinet! Who will have the courage to stand up and lead?'

One man in the audience had a question for Mr. Rabobank. He was from the Ministry of Economic Affairs (aka 'The Dutch Cabinet'), and he disagreed. It seemed the men knew each other. What followed was a heated debate. Mr. Cabinet defended his record, the Dutch model, and the idea of Dutch leadership. And then the retort from Mr. Rabobank: 'So why haven't you done anything to lead us out of this crisis, or to unify us for the reforms you promised, or – on immigration – to offer an alternative to saying "Full is Full?"' There was no answer.

The moderator then gave the mic to the other members of the panel. And then: 'Mr. Gregory Shapiro, what's your opinion?' Gulp.

At that point in the seminar, I must admit, I had more questions than answers:

- ✔ How can the Dutch be so independent-minded, yet also so obsessed with consensus?
- ✔ How can the Dutch be so liberal and open, yet also so Calvinistic and conformist?
- ✔ How can the Dutch be so proud about their identity, but then be so quiet about it?
- ✔ More to the point: what on earth am I going to say to ease the obvious onstage tension about immigration?

I took the mic, and I said, 'I think Máxima may have been misquoted. I think what she was trying to say is actually the same thing I learned in my assimilation course. For a small country, Nederland is surprisingly diverse. In fact, for me it's inspiring that so much of Dutch history is based on immigration. Some of the most famous Dutch names are imports: René Descartes, Baruch Spinoza, even William of Orange, who came "from German blood."'

The rest of the panel agreed. By the time the rest of the panel had spoken, a consensus had become clear. While the elder Dutchmen would still be debating whether Dutch culture is worthy or not, there are new Dutch people from all over the world, who like what Nederland stands for.

I realize there are many Dutch people who worry about too much immigration. As an American, let me put it like this: if you don't want so many immigrants, then stop being so awesome.

Adez

Want a health drink in the Netherlands?
It's pronounced *AIDS*.

CHAPTER 2

Dunglish

I worked with Unilever for 10 years, mostly in English. **– Mark Rutte, Prime Minister**

I suppose I am the textbook definition of an expat. I grew up in one country, I moved to another country, and I stopped. I came to the Netherlands for just one summer and thought, 'Nice country. Shame about the language…' But I stayed anyway. I came for work, I stayed for love, and – when I have to – I speak the language. Kicking and screaming, I took various Dutch language courses, and I eventually ended up in *Nederlands als Tweede Taal, Niveau 4*. Then I received a certificate that I'd effectively passed my assimilation course. *Tjakka!*

My wife says I have a love / hate relationship with the Dutch language. I think that's not fair. I'd call it hate / hate. To me, speaking Dutch is like giving a toast at a party while drunk: I embarrass myself every time. Yet, somehow, I keep doing it.

Some Dutch people seem to think the Netherlands is being overrun by waves of immigrants. I don't think so. The Dutch language acts as a natural deterrent. As the Dutch dunes protect us from the waves of the sea, we are protected from the waves of immigrants by the Dutch language. Tell anyone getting off the boat, '*Goedemiddaggggg*!' And most of them will get right back on the boat.

I fully recognize and respect the right of Dutch people to demand that I learn their language. But in practice, as soon as I speak Dutch to them, they quickly beg me to stop.

I start out making sense. But as the words get longer and longer, I'll get lost.

I'll try to say: 'I went to university, I'm reasonably intelligent, and I've studied foreign languages.'

What comes out in Dutch: 'I am to have the universe. I am intelligence. Study! I strange.'

I'd like to apologize to anyone who has ever had to listen to me speak Dutch. Indeed, I've studied foreign languages, but it never really stuck. What did really stick was my theater training. That means I'm quite good at approximating the *sound* of a language. And I'll be eager to try it out. But I still have no idea how to actually make sense.

When I speak Dutch, so I'm told, I sound authentic enough that Dutch people assume I'm a native speaker. Who may have a head injury. I speak Dutch to Dutch people, and they look at me with a mixture of pity and revulsion. Their look seems to say, 'Awww… you seemed to have an interesting idea at the beginning of that sentence. But now I think you're mentally disabled. Or mentally disturbed.' They look at me like you'd look at a dog with three legs. Or at a well-dressed man who pukes on himself in public.

My comprehension of Dutch is 'best good' (which is Dutch for 'neither best, nor good'). But the Dutch I speak is what I call 'Google Translate Nederlands.' 'ALL words the required ARE in sentence located. BUT the order in correct NOT to be seems.'

In the Netherlands, 'imperfect Dutch' is called *steenkool Nederlands*. What I speak is more like '*teenkrul Nederlands*.' My Dutch will make your toes curl.

Of course English can also be brutal, and there are plenty of wonderful books about that.

You've heard the story of the Dutchman who tells the Brit, 'I like to fuck horses.' I've also heard the one about the Dutchman who walks into a British furniture store and asks for a baby bed, using the Dutch word *ledikant*. To the Brits, the man was asking for a 'ladyc_nt.' And he was arrested.

But in Dutch you can come so close to making sense... and then there's that one false word that throws everything off. In a Dutch train compartment, if someone has motion sickness, I'll volunteer to sit facing backwards. Once, I said '*Geen probleem achterop te rijden*.' And I waited for people to stop laughing at the image of me hanging off the back of the train.

When I sit down to eat, I'll try to say 'Enjoy your food, everyone.' But I've accidentally added one tiny vowel sound, and instead I've said, 'Chew your food with your mouth open.'

I tried once to say, 'The school administration has deferred their decision.' But instead of *uitgesteld*, I said *ongesteld*. And I'd unwittingly announced that the entire administration was menstruating.

Sometimes the misunderstandings occur in plain English. Back when Seth Meyers was at Boom Chicago, we used to improvise with a character called Captain Technology. Together with his sidekick, he'd take complicated problems and make them simple. His sidekick would be played by a volunteer from the audience. In developing the game, we needed a name for the sidekick. As a reminder to 'keep things simple,' we called the sidekick 'Kid Simple.' As Americans, we had no idea there was a double meaning.

The first few times we did 'Captain Technology,' we got an American volunteer, and there was no problem. Volunteers onstage mostly play along and try not to take too many chances. So imagine our surprise when we got a British guy onstage to play Kid Simple, and he made a character choice I'd describe as 'mildly retarded.'

Someone explained afterward, 'in the UK *simple* means *retarded*.' Somehow, we still didn't change the name. The next night we got a Dutch volunteer onstage. 'I'm Captain Technology,' said Seth. 'And you're my sidekick Kid Simple!' The Dutch guy went on to play a sidekick who was part retarded, part deaf-mute and part spastic. He really committed. It ruined the scene, but it was hilarious. The poor guy was just doing what he was asked.

*

We're raising our kids to be bilingual. Mama speaks her native tongue with the kids, and Papa speaks his language. If I try practicing Dutch at home, it's my kids who cover their ears and say 'Papa, stop!'

Luckily, most Dutch people speak English pretty well. But of course they don't like to brag about it.

I'll ask a room full of Dutch people: 'How many of you speak English really well?'

They'll make ho-hum noises and stare at the floor.

Then I'll ask: 'How many speak English better than French people?'

And watch those hands pop up.

'... Better than German people?'

Even more!

There are many Dutch people who speak better English than some American people. And most of Glasgow.

Why do the Dutch speak English so well? In my experience, there's one reason: *ondertiteling*. Subtitles.I don't know why, but the biggest countries in Europe only have *Nasynchronisering*. Voiceovers.

And yes, it's hilarious. I'll turn on a TV in Germany and hear Mr. T. say, *'Ich wird nicht in kein flugzeug.'* As an American, I'm left to wonder: 'When did Mr. T. make a Nazi movie?'

But meanwhile in Nederland, you can hear the original Mr. T. say: 'I ain't going in no airplane, FOOL!'
And you can see the Dutch subtitle: *'Ik ga liever niet in dat vliegtuig, HOOR.'* This translates literally to: 'Listen, I'd rather not go in the aircraft.'

Not exactly right, is it? So, while subtitles can be very educational, the accuracy is questionable.

My wife learned English largely through subtitles. She'll tell you there is a real danger of Dutch people who did the same. You can pick them out easily. They're the ones who say 'Yes, I am perfectly The Englisch to be speakink.'

Just as I speak 'Google Translate Dutch,' there are some Dutch people who speak Google Translate English.

I once had to interview Amsterdam Mayor Eberhard van der Laan onstage. It was an English-language event, but he insisted on speaking Dutch. Offstage he told me, 'My English is okay, but I had a speech coach who told me, "There's nothing more dangerous than Dutch people who think they can speak English *fluid*."'

The previous Mayor was more ambitious. Mayor Job Cohen appeared in Stadsschouwburg to introduce Rev. Jesse Jackson, and he spoke English. He came out, and instead of saying 'Good evening, good evening,' he said, 'Good night, good night.' He got a huge laugh. And he smiled, as if to say, 'I guess I'm funny.' But we were in the audience thinking, 'That was the shortest speech ever…'

And then there's Prime Minister Mark Rutte. He is a role model for all of us Dunglish speakers. Rutte said, according to *De Volkskrant*: '*Tsja, ik heb 10 jaar bij Unilever gewerkt, daar ging veel in het Engels. Als je probeert je taal aan te passen, gaat dat vaak ten koste van je snelheid van denken.*'

In essence, Rutte admits to thinking partly in English. He's known for speaking Dutch with English phrases thrown in, like 'You win some, you lose some' and 'Old School.' These are okay, since there's no real Dutch translation. But he'll also throw in terms like 'Treasure chest,' for which there is a perfectly good Dutch term: *schatkist*. He's clearly favoring English here.

Prime Minister Rutte has been under pressure to use less English, which can be hilarious. Sometimes you can tell he's still thinking in English but translating back to Dutch. He once referred to a minister in his Cabinet as a member of his '*administratie*.' Why would he use that term? Perhaps because he'd been to America, where the President's team is known as the 'administration.' But in the Netherlands, '*administratie*' means bookkeepers – aka 'bean counters.' While this may be largely true, he didn't mean to actually say it.

Asked to eradicate Dunglish from his vocabulary. Rutte replied '*Ik doe mijn best…* but it's a tall order.'

*

Ik praat wel nederlands, hoor. I speak Dutch. But if I'm being honest, I don't like to speak Dutch. It makes my mouth feel sad.

There are things I like about the Dutch language. Dutch people's names can be very entertaining. With a straight face, they'll introduce themselves as Freek and Tjerk. Joke and Taco, Floor and Sander. Job and Bas. Fokko and Sikko.

I like that – when in doubt – you can put a diminutive suffix on just about anything. It's cute that the official word for cookie is *koek*, but everyone says *koekje*. Who wants a house, when you can have a *huis-je*? And a tree: *boom-pje*. And a pet: *beest-je*.

What does it say about Dutch culture? Maybe it has something to do with growing up next to a big sibling like Germany. Some people call it an inferiority complex. But that's not quite it. While some cultures – say America's – like to 'Think Big,' the Dutch language forces you to celebrate scaling down.

A Dutch friend has a boat. Coming from America, I ask 'Is it big?' He says 'No, it's a *boot-je*.'

I've heard Dutch people point to a map and refer to an entire country as a *land-je*. And it's quite common to hear Dutch people refer to the sun – *zon* – with a diminutive. The largest object in the solar system, and the Dutch call it *zonnetje*.

I'll still try to speak proper Dutch, but I admit it can be frustrating for everyone. I have a Dutch neighbor who teases me about my bad Dutch. In English. The other day, he wondered aloud, 'Why do I keep speaking English to you?'

Why indeed? Here are a couple of ideas:

1 You obviously enjoy it. Perhaps due to...
2 Aesthetics. English doesn't make you sound like an angry choking victim.
3 Population. Dutch is pretty far down the list of relevant languages in the world. English (including non-native speakers) is #1.

I respect that there is a Dutch language. I tolerate the Dutch language. But in truth I enjoy the Dutch language about as much as Geert Wilders enjoys immigrants.

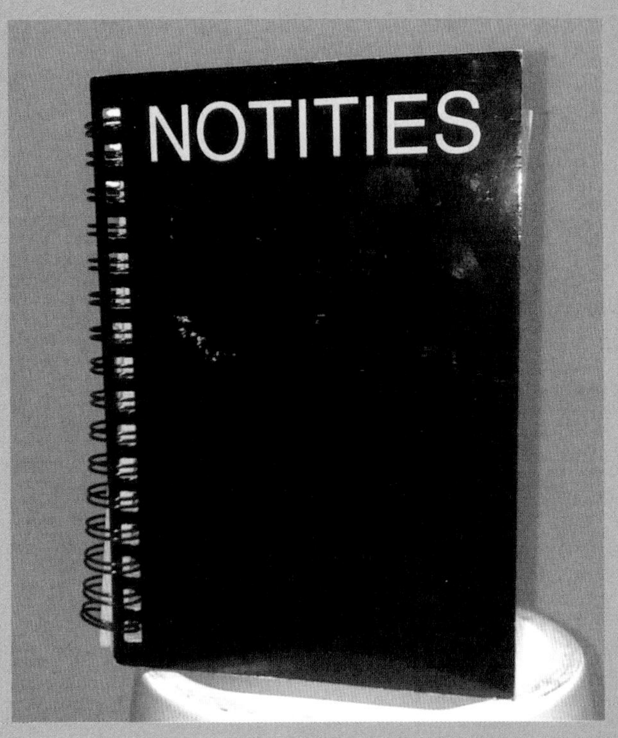

Notities
You can draw anything you like,
but NO TITTIES.

CHAPTER 3

Dutch Culture for Dummies

The Netherlands is such an advanced country they like to update their racism. First it was Indonesians, then Surinamese, now it's Turks and Moroccans. I like to think they have an official drawing, like when they pick the Olympics: 'From now on, we'll all be hating… Belgium. – Tom Rhodes, comedian

If you fly to the Netherlands on KLM and read about the Dutch in *The Holland Herald*, you may not realize that *Holland* is not the name of the country. You may be similarly confused by the Foreign Ministry ('Holland' logo) or the viral ad campaign 'Holland, the Original Cool.' In fact, there are 12 provinces here, and ten don't have *Holland* in the title. This gets pointed out within 1.5 seconds, when you say 'Hello, Holland' in, say, Brabant. It's understandable that most Dutch don't want to be called 'Holland.' *Hol* translates to *hollow*. And while Americans can be shallow, at least we're not *hollow*.

The name *Holland* also seems confusing to certain Dutch people, for example the Dutch national football team. Every two years, the stadiums are full of orange fans, yelling 'Hol-land! Hol-land!' But that only really refers to two provinces: Noord-Holland and Zuid-Holland. What about the players from the other ten provinces? What if they pass the ball to the guy from Friesland? He thinks, 'I'm not from either Holland' and misses. It must be so frustrating they feel like kicking some Spanish player in the chest.

In the assimilation course, we also got to learn the Dutch National Anthem: 'Het Wilhelmus.' It starts: '*Wilhelmus van Nassouwe, ben ik van Duitsen bloed…*'

I was the one in class raising my hand after the first line: 'I'm translating on the fly here, but is the opening line to your national anthem "I'm William, Founder of your country, and by the way I'm German?"'

And then came my follow-up question: 'Are there any other countries that start their national anthem by name checking another country?'

Not that we could think of. Can you imagine if America would do that?

'O say can you see – our British history? And Canada's nice. And a shout out to Mexico.'

And the Dutch anthem gets weirder. The end of the first stanza is basically: 'My allegiance for all time I pledge to the King of Spain.'

The anthem starts out by naming two other countries: Germany and Spain. And these are not just any two countries. As we learn in the assimilation course, these are countries that have invaded and occupied the Netherlands. Hence, the question: 'What kind of self-hating country has this as a national anthem?'

And don't forget, *Oranje* is *Orange*, which is in France. They might as well write, 'And don't forget Napoleon – he kicked our ass too.'

And no wonder the Netherlands don't do very well in the World Cup. How do they start off every international match? They sing 'Wilhelmus van Nassouwe…' Just when they should be trying to psych themselves up, they're thinking: 'We're going to win today! …Unless it's Germany or Spain.' That helps explain World Cup 1974 and 2010.

The Dutch Olympic team also seems affected by the odd Dutch anthem. Personally, I quite enjoyed the Dutch Men's Gymnastics champion Epke Zonderland. I happened to be watching the 2012 games with some people from the US and the UK. And – as there were no Dutch people around – I was happy to represent Nederland. After Zonderland won the gold, they asked me, '*Zonderland*. What does that mean?'

And I told them: 'Well… *zonder* means *without*. And *land* is land.' So Mr. Zonderland accepted the award for Nederland. But his name was saying, 'I'm not with them.'

*

As an American, I'm technically *allochtoon*. So are my kids. Then again, I realize the term *allochtoon* wasn't invented for people like me. Because we're 'Western.' And, I'm writing this in English. In fact, my third generation Moroccan neighbor speaks better Dutch than I do. But she gets called *allochtoon* and I don't. What are they really getting at?

As I understand it, '*allochtoon*' is a word Dutch people made up so that – if you can't pronounce it correctly – they know you're probably not one of them. I was introduced to the term *allochtoon* by a Dutch person, who explained, 'It's the opposite of *autochtoon*.'

What's *autochtoon*? (and why would you choose to call yourself that?)

'*Autochtoon* is someone born in the Netherlands.'

So it's like America and the way we use the word *foreigner*. As in: 'I don't trust them dang *FERners*.'

Allochtoon is a word that stays with you. If you're *allochtoon*, you can learn the language, assimilate, and even marry a Dutch person. Then after you have kids… they'll still be *allochtoon*. But THEIR kids… will still be *allochtoon*. After the fourth generation, well, maybe then they can be Dutch.

For a country based on tolerance and individual freedoms, it's odd the way the Dutch love pointing out people who are different.

The Amsterdam City Council has now placed a ban on the term in official business. According to the Amsterdam Integration Chairwoman Andrée van Es: 'Amsterdam will no longer be using the term *allochtoon*. We are all Amsterdammers, and from now on we will talk about Moroccan Amsterdammers or Turkish Amsterdammers.'

This is not the first time the Dutch have tried to replace the term *allochtoon*. Last time they tried '*Nieuwe Nederlander*.' It didn't catch on. Why? If you ask me; too many syllables. Now Amsterdam wants to change it to something largely unpronounceable, which will probably result in everyone still saying *allochtoon*.

Why not call people what they call themselves? In Amsterdam, I've heard Dutch Moroccans call themselves *Mocros*. I've heard Dutch Turks call themselves Turks. And if Dutch people call me a *Yank*, I won't be offended. In fact, legend has it that *Yankees* comes from the term *Jan-Kees*, so I'm half-Dutch already.

The *Inburgeringscursus* is an assimilation course designed to teach things about Dutch culture that most Dutch people don't know.

This assimilation course is very informative. Soon I was learning how to play 'Stump the Dutchie.' Why was the Treaty of Westphalia so important to the Dutch? My wife wasn't sure. Who was Johan Thorbecke? (Most Dutch people near Rembrandtplein think he's the patron saint of acute alcohol poisoning.) What's the most densely populated country in Europe? (It's not Nederland.)

'HEADSCARF IS A SYMBOL OF OPPRESSION'

I was the only tall, white male in my assimilation class. I was surrounded by people from Turkey, from Morocco, from Africa, Russia, Poland, and Romania. They were, according to a friend of mine, 'a United Nations of countries the Dutch don't want here.'

One of the biggest lessons I learned in the assimilation course wasn't about Dutch culture. It was about the other cultures. Every week, we'd find a partner and talk in Dutch about where we were from. I learned that the women in headscarves from Turkey had been to university in Istanbul and came over together to look for work / further their studies. I learned that the guy from Africa wanted to study water engineering here and return home to teach. I learned that the Moroccan woman wanted to start up a club for other Moroccan women to do fitness together. Most of them had already heard about the Dutch history of tolerance and immigration. In fact, that's why many of us moved here.

Our instructor was teaching us about the all-important Western values, such as the Freedom of Religion. We then learned that the headscarf is a symbol of oppression. We learned this while I was sitting next to six different women in headscarves. Awkward. One of the women raised her hand and said, 'Excuse, please. But – so you know – where I grew up, in Turkey, it was very secular society. Government rules were very strict. No headscarf allowed. So – for me – to move to the Netherlands and wear my headscarf, that is actually a symbol of liberation.'

The response: 'Sorry, but in this class that would be incorrect. If they ask you in the exam, just say it's a symbol of oppression.'

The most difficult part of the assimilation course was that I was being introduced to two different cultures at the same time: the Dutch culture of the textbooks; and the everyday Dutch culture I was seeing on TV.

Textbook: 'Tolerance is the foundation of Dutch identity.'
TV: 'Election Results Favor Right Wing. The Death of Tolerance.'

Textbook: 'Nederland is a country built upon consensus and the Polder Model.'
TV: 'Polder Agreement Rejected. The Polder Model is History.'

Textbook: 'Immigration has contributed to a rich and dynamic Dutch society.'
TV: 'Full is full!'

I was left to wonder, 'How do you teach about the Dutch identity when the Dutch are having an identity crisis?'

Nuts Support
When your underwear breaks down,
they deliver.

CHAPTER 4

Culture Shock Therapy

Durex ORGASMIC – Sex is fun!

– Condom package on drug store checkout counter, at eye level

Sex in the Netherlands is, frankly, annoying. Everyone thinks we're over here having sex all the time. In my experience, it ain't so. But the Dutch attitude toward sex can be useful. The Dutch treat sex as a natural part of life, which – for Americans – can be like Culture Shock Therapy.

When I moved here in the '90s, I remember there was a Safe Sex outdoor campaign on posters and billboards. Since the subject was sex, the poster showed a naked couple – about to have sex. The image was this: a woman kneeling on her bed, topless. Standing in front of her: a big, black dude, wearing nothing. With one hand, she's about ready to take off her panties, and with the other she's holding up a condom, saying '*Doe jij iets aan, doe ik iets uit.*' 'If you put something on, I'll take something off.'

To me, it was the perfect way of saying 'You're not in America anymore.' Granted, these days there is more sexually explicit imagery in America. And sometimes, there's even a little nudity. But both sexuality *and* nudity, combined with a black guy in a white girl's bedroom, would have many Americans calling the police.

And it's not just Americans. I was once hired by a Polish event organizer to do some standup for a corporate gig. She arranged the event at a posh hotel on Dam Square, which is also right next to the Red Light District. The instructions were clear: yes, you can talk to the audience, but don't mention the Red Light District. I asked the mostly male audience, 'What you want to talk about?' Unanimously, they answered, 'The Red Light District!' So – before I went on to talk about bikes and tulips – I did a couple of jokes mentioning the Red Light District. Immediately, the organizer went berserk. She flung herself into the tech booth in back, trying to wave me offstage – rather like a mother hen whose eggs had just been scrambled. She told the technician to cut my mic.

Afterward, I was furious. But she was furiouser. She was apoplectic. She stammered, 'I cannot believe you said those words… you have ruined the reputation of this city, of this country. You have killed a part of me… A part of me has died tonight.'

I hope she never saw that AIDS poster.

The Red Light District has been described as an adult-themed outdoor amusement park. And – like most amusement parks – if you've been through it once, you pretty much get it. Every time I'm hosting people from back in the States, they want to see the women in windows, the sex shops… and more than once I've had requests for the Casa Rosso live sex show. Or, as I like to call it, Bad Porn Live!

The live sex show keeps me guessing. Was it invented by someone who started in porn but loved live theater? Or someone from the theater, who really loved porn? Either way, they do put on a show. The partners are introduced rather like figure skaters: 'Let's hear it for Tony & Sabrina!' Like figure skaters, they have their chosen music and choreography – with many of the same poses figure skaters use. Except these guys go all the way.

The most interesting thing I ever witnessed at the live sex show was the moment they got an audience volunteer they weren't expecting. We were there with a group, mostly Americans and some internationals. There's a joke in the show when one of the couples stops in the middle of sex and asks for a volunteer. Nervous laughter usually follows. But that night, one of the women from our group stood up and said 'Pick me!' And sure enough, she got up onstage, got down on her knees and started going to work. I couldn't tell who was more mortified; the performers onstage or the group of Americans who – as it turned out – would never talk to her again.

By now, I've come up with a solution for my out-of-town guests: the sauna. The Dutch co-ed, naked sauna. It satisfies their need for nudity, and it's good for your skin. Also, it's Dutch Culture Shock Therapy in a nutshell. The first person who took me to the Dutch sauna was my Dutch boss. And she was very upfront about it. She said, 'This is the sauna, these are my tits, now everyone relax.'

I still remember telling my brother we were going to the Dutch sauna. He said, 'Oh no, I didn't bring my swimsuit.' That's how we do it in the States: hotel style. I told him, 'No problem. All you need is a towel.' But then in the locker room he was nervous. 'How can there be women in locker room?' That's the deal. You get undressed, they get undressed. And then he started enjoying himself: 'I'm going to see real naked ladies!'

But quickly there were so many naked females it was overwhelming. So many styles of pubic hair: The triangle, the stripe. The angry spider. Quickly he realized it's not just 'naked ladies.' It's all

kinds of naked people. Men, women. Young, old. Skinny, fat. Tattoos, appendectomy scars. And how often do you get to see Grandma naked? It's the real deal.

But for my brother, the real surprise was not the women. It was the men. He said, 'I've never seen so many penises before.' It was the length, but also the girth. The ones that grow and the ones for show. And the foreskins. Because – when you're from America, there are not a lot of foreskins. It's more like: 'Congratulations it's a boy' & snip snip. You're an honorary Jew.

In America, we've heard of foreskins. We just never get to see a lot of them. A gay friend of mine insisted that I study up: 'Foreskins are like fashion statements! They're like turtleneck sweaters, but there's such a variety. Some are form-fitting turtlenecks, that go right up over your head. Some are a little snug, and your head is always sticking out a bit. Some are hand knit with a *slurfje* that keeps on going. They're so cute! It's like Grandma just kept on knitting.'

I do appreciate that the sex industry is good business for the Netherlands. I've even had the pleasure of performing for one of their trade shows. Well, almost. Boom Chicago was hired to perform at an event called Europerve. It was all about latex, leather & PVC.

There was a runway and a fashion show for all the naughty garments. And then there was a duo act worthy of the Jim Rose Circus Sideshow. These people had so many piercings in their genitalia that they were able to combine magic, magnets and juggling. A poignant reminder that part of perversion is pain.

Unfortunately, I missed the early part of the show, because I had to perform in the home theater that night. But I didn't want to miss my colleagues in latex. Luckily, I did hear this first-hand account from my colleague Lesley:

'We'd all had appointments at some sex shop to be outfitted in sassy rubber duds. There was a generous amount of talcum powder required to wriggle into them … There we were, in a room full of angry-looking rubber-clad people shifting their weight from side to side, staring at us, and for the most part, silent. (In defense of the guy down front, it's hard to yell out a location with a ball gag in your mouth.) Mercifully, it was soon over and we were free to watch the rest of the show: a woman who shoved a Barbie Doll up her backside followed by another who swung a flaming cannon ball from her labia.'

I was given a ticket if I wanted to come later, just to see the spectacle. But it was a theme party, and I needed a costume. And so – like Cinderella going to the ball – I found my fairy godmother in the form of Frank the house manager. The man is an artist. Using the theme 'perve,' he looked around the theater for inspiration. Instead of a pumpkin, he found some plastic flowers and a plastic cactus. It helped that his surname was Plant. The plastic cactus was the size of a squat basketball.

He said, 'This is your costume.' He cut out a hole for my face to stick through, and he placed the cactus ball over my head. He took the cut-out remainder and made it into a codpiece, which I strapped on to my loins. The finishing piece was nothing but some sandals and a cape. To this day, I will think of myself as the belle of the Europerve ball.

The Dutch treat sex as a natural part of life, which I find reasonable. The way Americans treat sex, they find laughable. I was at the bar after a show once, and a couple Dutch women were talking about their American friend. The American woman had apparently said: 'I've been dating this guy for a few weeks. And I'm thinking of inviting him to bed.'

The Dutch women thought this was crazy: 'Why would you spend three weeks on a guy, if he might be crappy in bed?'

In America, it's: 'Take me to dinner, then maybe you can take me to bed.'

In Nederland, it's: 'Take me to bed, then maybe we can go to dinner.'

Culture Shock Therapy in a nutshell.

Anti Klit Shampoo

Misogyny in a bottle.

CHAPTER 5

My Multi-Culti Nightmare

Nederland has become a multi-culti nightmare.
– Geert Wilders

I was watching a speech by Amsterdam Mayor Eberhard van der Laan, who quoted a survey about the diverse population in Amsterdam. Apparently, there are more nationalities represented in Amsterdam than in any other city in the world (even Manhattan, which has the United Nations).

According to the Mayor, there are 180 nationalities living there. He used the number 180, because one study reported 179 nationalities, while a different study found 181. My theory is there's one guy from Burkina Faso, who's dating someone from Uruguay. But she lives in Utrecht. So when he stays over at her place, it's 179. But when she stays at his place, it's 181.

My neighborhood is in the Old West of Amsterdam. My American friends like to tease me: 'You live in The Old West? Are there gunfights at high noon?'

I tell them, 'No, that's '*Nieuw* West ...'

But it's true there are a lot of people here named *Shariff*.

On my street, I see both headscarves and white-haired Dutch retirees. I see Muslim women wearing 'the *hijab*,' and I see Dutch women wearing 'the *rain-scarf*.' Not much difference, really. If there's any one type of person who's a problem for me, it's the one who doesn't clean up after the dog.

My street is a nice mix of renters & owners, immigrants & natives, married & single. There are no daily riots. There are bike riders & car drivers, boat owners & poor folks, homo & hetero. Yet – as heterogeneous as it may be – the immigrants in my neighborhood are still in the minority. We have a lot of 'blank' people on my street: or – as the Dutch call them – The Dutch. There's no 'White Flight.' Otherwise we really would have to move to the suburbs.

I live next to a German artist, a Moroccan civil servant, a Pakistani taxi driver, a Turkish social worker, an Indonesian architect, a Surinamese deliveryman, an Italian telemarketer, an African city worker, a Ukrainian klezmer musician, and a Dutch film editor with a stutter. If any neighborhood qualifies as a multi-culti nightmare, this might be the one.

One of the more recent arrivals in my neighborhood is a Russian guy, and he loves it that there's an American nearby. He announces it loudly whenever he sees me. 'Here comes the crazy American.' 'Look, it's the crazy American!' And: 'Look out, he's so crazy.' I asked him one day what he meant, and he explained: 'Grigory, you must realize that – to be American – you have to be crazy. You are taught that "Life is Perfect," and it must become more perfect as you go on. This is crazy. In Russia we are taught "Life is a series of one disaster after another." ... And we are never disappointed.'

In terms of national stereotypes, these are the extremes: America ('Yay!') Russia ('Aww...') And in the middle there's the Dutch ('Ehhh...' accompanied by a shrug of the shoulders).

My analysis is: they can't be bothered, since – especially in Amsterdam – they've seen it all before. When you're known for tolerance, and you tell people to 'Just be yourself, you're crazy enough as it is,' then Crazy just leaves you Blasé.

- ✔ A building that looks like an enormous bathtub? 'Been there.'
- ✔ A man and a woman with their genitals pierced together? 'Seen it.'
- ✔ A guy in a G-string hanging over your table, while you're having a beer? 'Every time I go to Leidseplein.'

But all of a sudden, it was:

- ✔ 'A woman with a headscarf?' '*Doe normaal!* Just act normal!'

Yes, there are some troublemakers in my neighborhood. See if you can guess who's the biggest problem.

The Dutch Guy Next Door

Ronald moved in a few years ago, above the crazy Italian lady who would yell at my kids that they were playing too loudly. We were told he was an outpatient from a psychiatric facility, and that he had medical issues.

Normally, the amount of psychiatric outpatients allowed to live in one building is one. In the building next to us, we have two. On the first floor is a nice guy – as Dutch as they come and fitted with glasses designed in the '80s. In terms of his disability, he's a gentle soul. The only time we notice him is by his laugh from next door.

Apparently he likes watching 'Funniest Home Videos.' There's a lot of LOL.

Ronald was a different story. We weren't clear on what kind of disability he had, but you could tell life hadn't been treating him well. In his thirties, he looked like he was already in his fifties. Stubble on his face and stubble on his bald-ish head. He had sunken, dark eyes that darted around with an infectious nervousness. He wore camos & hoodies with an Ajax scarf, dressing as if trying to be accepted as an Ajax hooligan. Whether they would have him or not was unclear.

And he had a dog. A cute little dog, the kind kids love. My kids. They'd rush over to the dog to pet him. But as soon as they'd encounter Ronald's crooked smile of mismatched teeth and his fanatic gaze, even the kids knew this dog was going to be off-limits.

As soon as he moved in, he began with the charming habit of locking his bike to other people's bikes. He had enormous saddle bags on the sides of his bike, since – aside from receiving a disability allowance – he apparently 'delivered things' on the side. Already the chatting among neighbors began.

Part of Ronald's disability became clear when the fire trucks arrived one evening. Ronald was an epileptic. On the third floor. Every time he'd have a seizure, they'd need the crane from the fire department to airlift him down to the ambulance. And the police car for good measure. Our street is regularly filled with red lights, blue lights, orange too. It's festive, but not very practical.

Clearly this inopportune living situation would have to be remedied immediately. Who puts an epileptic on the third floor? We were told that the housing corporation from next door would have to relocate Ronald. We were told the same after his next seizure. And the one after that…

And then came 1 January, 2009. We greeted the New Year with a friendly ring of the doorbell, as Ronald came to tell us that his house was on fire, the fire trucks were on their way, and could we watch his dog? Apparently, he'd 'done something with the heater.' He didn't know what had happened, but it was on fire. Luckily, the fire did not spread. Our building was not affected, aside from the charming, lasting smell of smoke. Happy New Year! We spent a large part of New Year's Day evacuated from our home. It would not be the first evacuation.

In 2010, the police rang our doorbell in the middle of the night, telling us not to leave the building. At least we weren't being evacuated. Ronald was apparently on the roof, threatening to jump. The anti-suicide counselors needed our stairway to get to him. Our upstairs neighbor came home late and tired, and he couldn't get into his house due to the police perimeter. He spent the night at the police station.

Meanwhile, the fire trucks and ambulances were showing up regularly, every time Ronald would have an epileptic attack. It was bearable. But then came the telltale signs that the situation was becoming increasingly unstable. We'd noticed the cigarette butts in our garden for a while. No one in our building smokes, and we had a pretty good idea they were coming from next door. Then came larger objects: beer cans, failed carpentry projects, broken glass jars. And it was worse for the guy who lived on the ground floor directly under Ronald. He reported that dog poop was being tossed into his garden, as well as more disgusting items.

Then came the growing flow of people ringing our doorbell looking for Ronald. At first it was students. They'd heard of someone renting out a fourth floor apartment. Of course, it's illegal to use the fourth floor storage as living space. And it's certainly illegal to rent it out, when you're renting yourself. But apparently Ronald wasn't doing that. He was only advertising the space, taking the security deposit, and then not answering the door.

At the time, we didn't know what was causing these people to keep ringing our doorbell. But we did notice that they started getting weirder. Lost people hanging around on our stoop, asking 'Have we seen Ronald? The guy with the dog?' Apparently, Ronald had a drug habit, and he'd fallen behind in his payments. He also had a habit of paying for sex with some lovely transvestites, who claimed that he had not paid them either. And did we have any money to cover for our neighbor? We told the kids not to give any money to transvestites if they come to the door. In fact, we said, just don't answer the door. And did I mention that Ronald was HIV positive?

We found out Ronald was HIV positive the night he threatened to blow up the building. Apparently the police were onto him, they'd been pressuring him, and one night he broke. First, he blockaded the door. Then he smashed his front window and yelled down that he had a knife, he was cutting himself with it, and if anyone tried to get in, he'd infect them with HIV. Still, the police didn't evacuate us just yet. We went to bed.

It was after midnight when Ronald revealed that he'd opened up the gas valve and was threatening to blow up the building. That was our cue! The policeman came to the door and asked us to please come out of the house immediately. Do not get dressed. Grab a coat and get out immediately. We spent the night in our father-in-law's car. We watched as the assault team assembled, went in, and brought him out. They did their job. No one was infected with HIV. And the only question was: what would happen to his dog?

The neighbor on the first floor watched the dog. The police later came to our door and explained what had been going on. Ronald remained in custody until he could receive a psychiatric evaluation. Apparently he passed, since he was back in his apartment the next week.

Next, the police came into our living room. They asked to hold a neighborhood meeting about Ronald. It was explained to us that it's extremely difficult to get someone committed to a psychiatric facility, even if this someone has a large file already. At least it was nice to get a bunch of us multi-culti neighbors together. We agreed: the multi-culti part is not the problem.

The German Artist & His Plants

German jokes still go over quite well in Amsterdam, and it would be easy to portray my neighbor as a punctual conformist with no sense of humor. But then there's another category of Germans called German Artists in Exile: that's my neighbor.

Walter is a tall, skinny, dark-haired artist in his fifties. 'The '50s' also describes his style of dress: he prefers a fedora hat and a long, wool coat, even in summer. I never see him *smoking* a joint, but it's obvious he's a pot-smoker from the amount of vowels he uses to greet me: 'Heeeeeey! *Buurmaaaaaaaan*!' Like many artists, he's got a lot of art lying around. His back yard is a small sculpture garden: a hand-carved chair, mosaic tiles on the ground, and a huge totem pole made of whalebone. The amount of attention that most people put into grooming themselves? That is the amount of attention Walter puts into his art.

Walter also has a green thumb. His bamboo is enormous. His front stoop features a number of climbing vines and a big honeysuckle plant. There's even new tree on the block, planted by Walter. In an act of civil disobedience, he flipped up a paving stone and stuck a tree in there. ('Isn't he German?' you ask. Don't forget: 'artist exile German.') In just a couple of years, his tree has exploded into a nicely large, green presence on our street. Every once in awhile I see a couple guys in civil servant outfits patrolling the neighborhood and taking notes. 'This tree is not on our map…' they say. And just before they start to dig it up, there's Walter out on the street, protesting with them to keep the green. I don't know how he does it, but the tree remains.

Across the street from us there is also a wall of ivy all the way up to the roof. At least there was. On the third floor there's a white-haired Dutch couple. (I call them Henk & Ingrid.) (I'll tell you why later.) One sunny Saturday they decided to rip all the ivy down. Apparently, they had complaints that the ivy was damaging their wall, and that rats were climbing up the vines into their windows. Never mind that the wall has no windows. Never mind that the wall they left behind is pockmarked, and gray, and is now constantly covered with graffiti. And never mind that – most perplex-

ingly – it's a rental building. They had no permission to rip down the ivy to begin with. But it's their country, so I guess we'll live with their norms and values: gray wall and graffiti. My favorite so far: 'Turks, go back to Morocco.'

Enter Walter. On another sunny Saturday not long after, Walter went off to the garden store. He snuck over to the building across the street and flipped up some more paving stones, right up against the building. And he plopped in a bunch of green and flowering plants. I watched as he wiped his hands and strolled back across the street toward me: 'Heeeey, hiiii. Nice eh?'

I looked again a few hours later, and I noticed Henk & Ingrid also digging around by their building. They had ripped up all of Walter's plants, and were throwing them in the dumpster. Walter went out to protest. It was too late. Henk & Ingrid replaced the paving stones exactly as they were, recreating the perfectly straight lines. So who's being the Nazi here?

The Pakistani Taxi Driver & His Wife & Kid

They live in the apartment next to us. The three of them are squashed into two rooms. Of course, the husband isn't around a lot. He works long hours, and we never see him. They speak Urdu to each other. To us, they speak Dutch. Her Dutch is coming along. Almost as bad as mine.

She is a real neighbor. She is not afraid to ring the doorbell, with her headscarf on and everything. And – even when it's not a good moment – there she is with a bowl full of chickpea soup. Or a snack made with crushed pistachios. Or dessert, involving sweet yoghurt and honey and sesame. I tell her: 'Come on in!' For me, these dishes are uncharted territory – not territory I'd recommend for everyone. And, if they'd be on a menu, let's say I wouldn't order them from a menu. But they are certainly delicious to try, and we have to appreciate the generosity.

Their generosity seemed inversely proportional to their income. I wondered aloud if it might be a good idea to return the favor. My wife and I cooked up the idea to cook up something typically Dutch. I decided on the traditional dish of *Witlof / ham-kaas* – an oven dish featuring potatoes with Belgian endive, covered with ham and cheese.

If you haven't spotted the inherent flaw in this plan, you are like I was. I brought my dish out of the oven and proudly touted it over to the neighbors, ringing the doorbell and offering my gift with gusto. My neighbor took one sniff at it and turned away in disgust. 'Is that… pork?'

Yes, I'm the guy who brings a steaming-hot dish full of ham into a Muslim woman's house, as a gesture of thanks. In a previous life, I would have been the one offering blankets to Native Americans ('pardon the germs'). If there is a problem in our neighborhood, perhaps the enemy is us. The good news is: in terms of Dutch culture, I guess I'm fitting right in.

Vague Coiffures
Really unspecific hair care.

CHAPTER 6

Waste Not

How do you make copper wire? Put a copper penny in a room with a couple Dutchmen and watch them fight over it.
– My uncle (who is Jewish)

There's something charming about the stereotype that Dutch people are cheap. I think it's the fact that the Dutch seem to really believe it about themselves.

But are the Dutch really cheap? Or is it something else? Perhaps they're *zuinig*. I realized the difference when I went to visit my Dutch mother-in-law. She lives right on the border of Limburg, and every time we show up, she serves us fruit pie *vlaai*. I dutifully balance the tiny plate on my knee, as she also offers me a cup of coffee on its saucer. And just when I've managed to balance all that, in comes the cookie tin. If anything, she's generous to a fault. Not exactly cheap.

It was when she offered the cookies that it happened. One time, after I chose a cookie, she slammed the cookie tin shut almost aggressively. And I thought: 'Ha! I've got you!'

I said, teasingly, 'So, it's just like they say in the books. You're cheap with those cookies!'

She asked, 'What do you mean?'

I explained, 'You closed the cookie tin so quickly. You must want to make sure I don't take more than one!'

And she said, 'No, no... I close the cookie tin so that – when you want another cookie – the cookies, they are fresh.'

And I thought, 'Wow, that's a different way of looking at it... You actually care about quality.' Come to think of it, I come from a culture where the cookies stay open until they're quickly devoured. But the idea of Quality? Efficiency? We just take one look at what happens here and conclude: 'CHEAP.'

If anything, sometimes the Dutch take the freshness concept a bit too far.

Me: 'Where's my bread?'

My colleague: 'What bread?'

Me: 'The bread I bought and put here in the refrigerator.'

My colleague: 'There was no bread.'

Me: 'I bought it yesterday. A full loaf of bread.'

My colleague: 'Oh, that old rubbish! I threw it out.'

You call this cheap? They're more wasteful than the Americans.

The Dutch are so fanatic about fresh bread that they make it nearly impossible to *buy* fresh bread. The supermarkets do their best, building in little mini-bakeries in every store on every block. But even though the ovens are constantly churning, the fresh stuff is frequently sold out. Of course, there's always a plentiful supply of 'factory bread,' which my wife refuses to buy. My wife abhors any

preservatives with her food, including the preservative known as 'the refrigerator.'

No, if bread is kept at all, it must be kept at room temperature until it is Not-Quite-Fresh bread. And Not-Quite-Fresh bread must be thrown out. And if you take the trouble to throw your breadcrumbs to the birds, they assume you must be Muslim. The front page of *Het Parool* recently stated that the amount of food discarded by Amsterdam each day could feed a small city. (The fact that Amsterdam IS a small city proves that *Het Parool* really is Amsterdam's newspaper.)

When I first came to Nederland, there were so-called 'GFT' bio-waste bins in every home. Anything biodegradable would go in the bins, the city would pick them up, and no need to waste the bread. In practice, everyone used the things only once. They got manky. And then everyone started using them as normal garbage cans. Then came the friendly-reminder posters and leaflets: 'Say, neighbors, metal isn't a vegetable!' And soon after that, the city apparently became fed up.

Since then, there are no bio-waste bins. Yet the city of Amsterdam does a rather good job of reminding you how green they are by running things on 'green energy.' The trams, for example, run on electricity from turbines powered by the incinerator of all the food we throw away. So it's a bit green, I suppose.

I remember staying at a house in France for a week. They had garbage containers, but there wasn't much left to put in them. We were encouraged to separate out our glass, our paper, metal and four kinds of plastic. Plus the house had its own compost bin. After all that, we didn't need a 'garbage can.' In the Netherlands – at least in Amsterdam – they do collect paper, glass and sometimes plastic. The sparse few bins I've seen for recycling plastic are usually overflowing, resulting in mounds of plastic being dumped next to the bin, hence all over the street. Better to burn it, apparently. Gotta keep them trams running.

The promising innovation is the grease truck. Apparently the used fat from the deep-fryers in fast food restaurants and snack shops can be recycled and refined into biofuel.

In fact, KLM is now running trans-Atlantic flights on trans-fats. Innovative? Yes. Efficient? Yes. So you can't call the Dutch cheap.

If you want a new understanding of the word *zuinig*, look no further than the favorite candy of the Netherlands: *drop*. I assume the reason it's called *drop* is because it's the flavor I usually drop on the floor at the movies. I hold it up to the screen, and if the light doesn't shine through: Drop. It's black licorice. The least favorite flavor in most parts of the world is the most popular here. And there are so many different varieties of this odd flavor: hard, soft, sweet, salty. It's the salty candy I really can't understand. There are some types of drop I would describe as 'Industrial Accident Flavor.'

My wife constantly tries to convert me. She thinks someday I'll 'come to my senses' and realize *drop is lekker*. We'll be driving on a road trip, and she'll say 'Want something tasty?' Then she'll plop it in my mouth, and my senses are so assaulted, I almost steer us off the road into a ball of flame. My reaction is partly because of shock, and partly because – after tasting black licorice – my body shuts down and wants to stop tasting anything ever again.

I couldn't understand why the Dutch love *drop* so much. I looked at the ingredients: Sugar. Anise flavor. And gelatin. But what is gelatin? I did a corporate show for the makers of gelatin. And according to their annual report, it's:
– cow hooves
– cow bones
– cow teeth
+ a new innovation: 'Fallen animals.'

I had to ask, 'I'm sorry: what are fallen animals?'
It turns out they're the ones that are normally too sick to eat. It used to be that when they'd fall over and die, you'd have to throw them out with the bread. But now – thanks to a new industrial process – when they drop, the Dutch make *drop*.

There's never been a better example of 'waste not, want not' than *drop*. Not since the early Native Americans, who famously used 'all parts of the buffalo.' They used the skin to make their shoes. They used the hide to make their tents …

If you gave the Dutch the chance to dress up in *drop*, they probably would:

'Look at my hat, made of drop! Look at my earrings, made of drop!'

And no wonder Zwarte Piet is so popular. His face looks like *drop*.

But you can't call the Dutch cheap.

If the Dutch were really cheap, then would they be so extravagant with their public sculpture? These metal tree stumps can be found in the Amsterdamse Bos forest. At some point, the city must have had a sack of money to plant some new trees, perhaps in an area that needed more trees. But no – instead, there was an artist who said 'I have an idea! Why not make people think about *dead* trees?' Less green, more death. If you can afford to think this way, you're not exactly cheap.

This sculpture is near my kids' school. It's a sculpture of a man. How can you tell it's a man? Because of the huge, spiky steel erection. In an era when we're cracking down on inappropriate content for children, why would we pay money for sculptors to visually abuse us and our children?

This sculpture was commissioned for the opening of a public building in Amsterdam Oud West. Integrated into the façade of the building is a series of white ladders extending up and out and high above the street. At the top of the ladders is a life-size human figure with its arms stretched up to the heavens. And it's called 'How to Meet an Angel.' What is the public building that received such a sculpture? It's a mental health center for people with psychiatric problems. I'm not sure if the sculptor intended it to be used as a suicide diving board. But one thing is clear: if the Dutch can afford public art like this, then you can't call the Dutch cheap.

Moto Dick
Strangely, it’s not a sex shop.

CHAPTER 7

IT'S THE LITTLE DIFFERENCES

It's the little differences. I mean, they got the same shit over there that we got here, but it's just... there it's a little different.

– Quentin Tarantino via John Travolta

Yes, there are little differences. But the differences are a little different since I got here.

I first came to the Netherlands in 1994. When the World Cup went to America, I came to Europe. It was the year Nelson Mandela became President, Wim Kok became Prime Minister, and Quentin Tarantino released *Pulp Fiction*. According to most Americans, 'Everything I Needed to Know about Amsterdam I Learned in *Pulp Fiction*.' Hash bars. Glass of beer in the movie theater. And *frites* with mayonnaise.

But it's interesting when you go back and look at the dialogue from the movie. Let's see how much of it still holds true.

Samuel L. Jackson: 'So tell me again about the hash bars in Amsterdam.'

STOP. 'Hash bars?'

Amsterdam has never had '*hash bars.*' There are '*coffeeshops,*' a term which is so misleading that Tarantino had to change it for the American market. Ah, those little differences. Americans also have their fair share of idiosyncratic euphemisms, such as 'drugstore' where you go to get medicine. So it's funny when I hear US tourists ask Dutch people for the '*drugstore,*' and they're directed to the '*coffeeshop.*'

(See also: Brits asking for 'the Boots' and being directed to the shoe stores on the Leidsestraat.)

Travolta: 'Okay, what you wanna know?'
Jackson: 'Hash is legal there, right?'
Travolta: 'Well, yeah it's legal, but it ain't 100% legal.'

STOP. 'Hash is legal?'

In fact hash is 100% IL-legal. The Dutch choose not to enforce it. In 1994 they also chose not to enforce soft drug rules, and for a while there were smart shops selling actual dried mushrooms... until a French girl jumped off a building. Now, dried mushrooms are unheard of! (Unless you ask for 'truffles'.) In 1994, the only things that were illegal AND enforced were ecstasy and cocaine. Now you can't bring a pack of gum into a dance event without a lecture and a patdown by the special frisking police.

Travolta: 'You can't just go into a restaurant and start puffing away... They want you to smoke it in your home or certain designated places.'

Jackson: 'And those are the hash bars?'

STOP. 'Puffing away?'

Yes, those are the hash bars. As long as – since 2007 – the hash bar has a smoking section. Why do we need a smoking section? To protect all the people who don't smoke. What are you doing in a hash bar if you don't smoke? No one knows.

Travolta: 'Like when you go to see a movie in Amsterdam, you can take a beer into the movie theater. And I ain't talking about no plastic cup neither. I mean a glass of beer.'

STOP. 'Glass of beer?'

Nowadays rarely a glass of beer, but longnecks are plentiful. I find this an improvement, actually. But did I mention that it's hard to find beer in the coffeeshop anymore?

Travolta: 'It breaks down like this: it's legal to buy it, it's legal to own it...'

STOP. 'It's legal?'

You can still buy weed at a coffeeshop, but you can't get beer. You can still get mushrooms at the smart shop, but you can't get dried mushrooms. Unless you dry them yourself, which apparently no one has thought of. You can get beer at a brown café, but if you want a café café, the coffee's not great. If you want good coffee, don't go to the coffeeshop; go to the CoffeeCompany, which is now the SaraLee Company. So you might as well go to Starbucks.

Travolta: 'And – if you're the proprietor of a hash bar, it's legal to sell it.'

STOP. 'Legal to sell it?'

But it's only legal if your coffeeshop is not within 500 meters of a school. AND if your coffeeshop is not too close to the border with Belgium. AND if you check the passports of the clientele to make sure there are no tourists. Because surely the innovative Dutch won't figure out that they can make a killing by buying the weed themselves and re-selling it to students and tourists on the black market.

Travolta: 'But that don't matter, because – get a load of this. If the cops stop you in Amsterdam, it's illegal for them to search you. That's a right the cops actually don't have.'

STOP. 'Illegal for them to search you?'

Now they can search you whenever they want. And if they search you, you'd better have valid ID. Otherwise you can be arrested. These are the differences. And if you want to sit on a terrace to have a glass of beer, you can't do it while standing. You have sit inside the 'terrace-approved area.' Because if you're outside the 'terrace-approved area,' then the proprietor might get a fine. And if you want to just get out of town, you'd better have a light on your bike, otherwise *you* might get a fine. And you can't take a taxi without the taxi driver trying to beat you to death, but *he* won't get a fine. And wherever you go, you have to have valid ID. An ID with your photo on it. *UND your papers must be correct at all times.*

The little differences are a little different.

POT

Reinforcing every Dutch stereotype, it's the POT delivery van.

Chapter 8

How the Dutch See Themselves

Film is [a country's] ideology at its purest.
– Slavoj Žižek, philosopher

I dreamt I was in a crappy movie with Naomi Watts… no wait, that really happened.

One way to find out how a culture sees itself is to look at its cinema and directors. In the case of the Netherlands, the best-known directors seem like they're trying to be American.

As a teenager, I saw Paul Verhoeven's *Robocop,* which exploited the American cop-movie genre with such gleeful, gratuitous violence I couldn't watch the whole thing. Then Jan de Bont made *Speed,* a veritable homage to the Hollywood action movie. Next up for US success was supposed to be Dutchman Dick Maas.

Dick Maas has been making American knock-off films since the early '80s. I remember the boat chase in *Amsterdamned* along the famous canals. But after the hero goes crashing into the rowing club, then the Dutch street organ, then an even more implausible brass band flotilla … you're left wondering if Maas is taking it seriously or if he's taking the piss. Is it homage, or is it parody? To me Dick Maas is like the Dutch Ed Wood. The only way to enjoy his films is because 'they're so bad they're good.' Meanwhile, Maas continues making films for the Dutch (and Hollywood clearly prefers Dutchman Anton Corbijn).

Dick Maas' first-ever movie was *De Lift* in 1983. It was a simple horror story about an elevator where people were being killed – by the elevator. For everyone who's ever wondered what happens when you get your head caught between the elevator doors, this movie is for you.

In the late '90s, to make his big jump to the US market, Maas decided to redo his first movie, with a *Die Hard* makeover. The exteriors were filmed in Manhattan, but the bulk of the production took place in Almere (by the *Big Brother* studios). Since this time the movie was in English, they needed American actors. I went to the audition.

Everyone from Boom Chicago tried out for the film. Ike Barinholtz got to play a fussy office assistant. Josh Meyer (Seth's brother) was on a SWAT team. And I got a role as a tech nerd / computer expert named Chip (get it?). The filming was scheduled for August, 2000 – right in the middle of the Edinburgh Fringe Festival, where I was performing for Boom Chicago. We told them I probably couldn't do it, unless they could schedule all my scenes into the same 36 hours. Miraculously, they scheduled all my scenes into the same 36 hours. The next thing I knew I was on the set next to Naomi Watts. And I was the one being labeled as the 'prima donna.'

Being Dutch, Dick Maas puts the 'direct' in 'director.' As an actor, I enjoyed working with Maas. He was very up-front about what he wanted from the scene and what the story needed. Then again, Dick Maas is also a writer-director. As I'm an actor-writer, I was a bit confused. On set, my text was being taken very seriously, but my character was being portrayed in the broadest stereotypes possible. It was less 'character' and more 'caricature.' Maas personally dictated the details of my nerd costume: mismatched suspenders and tie, goofy glasses, and food stains on my shirt. I remember we had to do a retake to make sure there was enough pizza sauce on me. Were we making some ironic statement about stereotypes? No, it seemed more like Dick was just having fun, sticking in a joke whether it fit or not. Oh, well. It wasn't supposed to be high art.

But you have to give the man some credit for casting. At that point, I'd never heard of Naomi Watts. It was the year 2000 and we were all more impressed with her co-star James Marshall from *Twin Peaks*. James was open and friendly, and he liked having an American to talk to on the set. I joked with him, and I told him he didn't seem as dumb as his character on TV. He eagerly agreed. After *Twin Peaks*, he'd not only had to fight typecasting. He'd had to deal with a serious illness. The Dick Maas movie was to be his comeback and his 'big chance to play an intelligent role in a smart script.' Clearly, his agent hadn't seen any Dick Maas movies.

As for Naomi Watts, she was Australian. That's about all we knew. And I'd heard she'd grown up with Nicole Kidman. Naomi Watts had a great Australian accent. It's the accent I've heard Australians refer to as 'Strine.' But she was working on her American accent for the film. We'd be running lines, and in a flawless American accent, she'd say 'Chip, do you want a coffee?' And then she'd turn aside and ask, 'dizz thet sound roight?'

Thanks to Dick Maas, I'm proud to be able to say I helped Naomi Watts with her American accent. We had a couple scenes together. On-camera I played a nerd, and she played a smart, good-looking femme fatale who was way out of my league. Off-camera, our relationship was no different. Naomi Watts and me: you can see our chemistry onscreen for all of 90 seconds. If you look for the film on DVD… well, you won't find it. (Probably Naomi Watts' management saw to that.)

The remarkable thing about the film *Down* was its timing. In the script, written by Dick Maas, the killer elevator kills so many people that even the White House gets involved. The President calls it 'terrorism' and sends in commandos with stingers (anti-aircraft missiles). Of course, this was standard film script fodder for every movie that came out after September 11.

But here's the thing. Dick Maas' movie came out *before* September 11. A week before. *Down* opened on the 5th of September, 2001. For a week, it did rather well. But somehow, after September 11, no one wanted to see a horror movie set in Manhattan about people dying in skyscrapers.

Yet – for a film that came out before 9/11 – this Dutch guy Dick Maas came up with some incredibly prescient dialogue. Of course, Maas needed a missile launcher in his story to set up the obligatory explosion at the end. But how did he justify it? Here's some of the text.

Commando 1: 'Why do we need Stingers?'
Commando 2: 'Terrorists have airplanes too.'

And this bit:

Commando 1: 'Up we go.'
Commando 2: 'If you see Bin Laden, say hello.'

Say what you will about Dick Maas' movies, but he did kind of predict 9/11, the week before 9/11. In retrospect, I'm not sure if that's a credit to Dick Maas, or if it's because 9/11 was so predictable. Either way, the Netherlands is still stuck with him.

*

One of my first impressions of Dutch culture was a Dutch art house film I saw in Chicago. The film came out before I even knew I'd be moving here, so I suppose it must have made a good impression. *Spoorloos* featured a mild-mannered Dutchman who was also a sadistic killer. A very good first impression.

In America, we like our happy endings, even if it means a tacked-on, Hollywood ending.

Dutch movies don't have happy endings; Dutch movies just end. Boy meets Girl, Boy loses Girl, Boy and Girl get together for obligatory nude scene and have sex anyway. 'Do they live happily ever after?' Probably not.

Spoorloos is even better. [Spoiler Alert: I'm about to give away the ending to this movie you probably saw ages ago and don't quite remember.]

It's about a guy whose wife gets kidnapped. Actually it's not his wife. They're just 'living together,' because it's Nederland. Boy meets Girl, Boy loses Girl, Boy goes crazy looking for Girl. And he finally meets the guy who kidnapped her. He's this creepy Dutch family man with a pointy beard.

Pointy Beard says, 'You want to know what happened to your girlfriend? Well, I can't tell you. But I can show you.' The boyfriend is so desperate he says *yes*. He lets himself be drugged, and the screen goes black. The next thing we see is a lighter in the darkness. *Flick, flick.* And we hear the sound of dirt being shoveled onto a coffin. Our hero is being buried alive, just like his girlfriend. The end.

I'd never seen a movie like this before! In fact, it was a bit of a hit in America. Lots of people were talking about the film, saying 'Wow, the Dutch are hard core.' And of course, not long after, there was a Hollywood remake: *The Vanishing* with Kiefer Sutherland. It's a lot like watching any episode of 24 with Jack Bauer. He's desperate, looking for clues, torturing people. And then he meets the kidnapper (played by Oscar-winner Jeff Bridges) (whose Dutch accent wins the award for 'Worst-ever').

[Spoiler Alert: the rest is the same, shot by shot.] Our hero drugs himself, wakes up in a box, and flicks on his lighter. The only difference is it's America, so they had to use a big Zippo lighter.

But Hollywood did it – they killed the hero. Hard core! Then they tried the film in front of American test audiences, and the Americans said, 'I don't get it... How does he get out of the box?'

They explained: 'That's the whole point: He doesn't. Surprise!'

The test audiences still didn't get it: 'But how is there a happy ending?'

'There is no happy ending. It's about how desperate he was.'
'Oh, okay. ... But seriously, how does he get out of the box?'

So – of course – they filmed a different ending. Kiefer Sutherland is in the box. Jeff Bridges finishes shoveling the dirt. Cut to a new girlfriend who for some reason is driving around in the woods. Suddenly, she stops: 'Is that digging I hear?' She rushes into the middle of the forest and somehow, in the dark, she detects freshly turned earth. Then she's digging up our hero, she pries open the box, and there he is! ... But she's too late. He's already dead. Or is he? Our hero wakes up with a huge breath of relief and hugs his new girlfriend. Happy ending.

But wait – here comes the bad guy. He's got a shovel and wants to kill our hero. So they shoot him, and he's dead. Or is he? Just as they hug again, the killer wakes up and grabs the girlfriend, so that Kiefer Sutherland has to whack him with the shovel. He smashes Jeff Bridges' head in, drops the shovel and literally has to look into the camera and say 'It's over... It's over.' That's what it took for the American test audience to finally be satisfied: 'Okay! I guess it's over.'

Of course, for the Dutch market – if they had filmed a separate ending – the hero would have killed the bad guy, had sex with his girlfriend and then died.
'Do they live happily ever after?' Probably not.

Firezone
I guess the name '*Flaming Death Area*' was taken.

CHAPTER 9

Politician of the Year

I hope this kid doesn't come to me to extend his residence permit.
– Fred Teeven, State Secretary of Security and Justice

In the world of political standup comedy, there's one top gig: the White House Press Correspondents' Dinner. In Dutch politics there's no real equivalent. But I've come close. Every year *Het Parool* hosts an event called 'The Year in Politics,' and I was the host in 2011 – right after Geert Wilders took power... But I'll get to that in a minute.

One of the shows we do at Boom Chicago is 'Political PARTY.' We treat Dutch politics like Americans do: as an over-the-top celebration. Pep Rosenfeld and I co-host the show with pollster guru Maurice de Hond. Maurice invites his favorite Dutch politicians. Here's how it works:

- ✔ We interview the politician.
- ✔ We find out who's the politician's adversary.

- ✔ We make the politician dress up as that adversary and answer questions in character. AND I answer questions dressed up as the politician.

For example, one of our first guests was Femke Halsema (former head of the green political party GroenLinks).

- ✔ We interviewed Halsema.
- ✔ She said her adversary was Mark Rutte.
- ✔ She dressed up as Mark Rutte and answered questions.
- ✔ I dressed up as Femke Halsema and answered questions.

She did a pretty good Mark Rutte, and afterward she said it was a surprisingly liberating experience. Likewise for me. While she was busy making Rutte look ridiculous, I was free to make her look ridiculous.

It's one thing to stand in front of the US President and make jokes about him. But sitting next to a politician and doing an impression of her is not for the faint of heart. Someday, I hope to live up to the shining example of Stephen Colbert, who famously stood next to George W. Bush and ridiculed the President without him realizing.

Another one of our guests at 'Political PARTY' was Lodewijk Asscher. Back then he was Amsterdam Deputy Mayor. Now he's Deputy Prime Minister. His English was no problem. And somehow, in my experience, when politicians answer questions in their second language, they're a little more candid. Of course, we had to point out that Asscher's name doesn't translate very well into English. It starts with 'Ass' and ends in 'Chair.' But actually – for a civil servant – it's kind of perfect. We teased Asscher that he looked like the perennial young-man actor John Cusack. Cusack made *High Fidelity*, a fine film. And Asscher made a priority of improving school infrastructure, a fine move. But then came the North-South Metro line, which – like Cusack's *2012* – was WAY overbudget and deeply unsatisfying.

Lodewijk Asscher picked – as his adversary – (former PM) JP Balkenende. He entered with 'Folks, if you liked Balkenende 1–4 you're going to love Balkenende 5!' And – of course – I sat next to Asscher, doing my impression of Lodewijk Asscher. As it turned out, Asscher was not only a good improviser, but a good actor too. He didn't just do a simple Balkenende impression; he really got into character as Balkenende. He started debating as Balkenende. His Balkenende started attacking my Asscher as a 'Big Government Liberal.' Let's take a moment and give him credit for that. How many politicians are able to jump in and debate both sides of an argument? In retrospect, I guess it's a key criterion for anyone wanting to take part in Dutch politics: the art of compromise. More recently, Deputy Prime Minister Asscher has been busy with labor reform negotiations. And – as famous Sociologist Charlie Moskos used to say – you know it's a good example of a compromise when everyone is disappointed equally.

Perhaps our most unlikely guest at 'Political PARTY' was a man named Hero. Hero Brinkman was an MP in Geert Wilders' party PVV. Nervously, Pep Rosenfeld and I started out the show making a number of jokes about Geert Wilders and PVV:

- ✔ 'Geert Wilders is head of the PVV "Freedom Party," even though, under 24-hour protection, he has no freedom. It's kind of like George Bush starting up a Party for the Mentally Gifted.'
- ✔ 'Geert Wilders was named "Politician of the Year." Specifically, the year 1941.'
- ✔ 'Geert Wilders doesn't like headscarves, which is ironic because – if anyone could benefit from wearing a headscarf – it's Geert Wilders.'

Luckily, Hero Brinkman was not a fan of Geert Wilders either. At one point, Brinkman had been Number 4 on the party list. But, as Brinkman explained, when he started speaking out about the need for more democracy within the party, Wilders bumped him down to Number 14. According to Brinkman, the Freedom Party is not really a party, since there's only one official member: Geert Wilders. You may notice other political parties having meetings, voting on internal issues, electing members to party leadership... not so with the Freedom Party. That would apparently be too much freedom.

Brinkman would go on to split off and form his own party, creating yet another exotic item on the grand menu of Dutch politics. In America, we have over 300 million people and only two political parties. The Netherlands has just 17 million people but well over 17 parties. Apparently, the smaller the country, the more they like to disagree.

I once spoke at a private event for a bunch of former politicians. In attendance was former Prime Minister Ruud Lubbers. He was accompanied by former Immigration Minister Gerd Leers. Their eyebrows were fantastic. Gerd Leers has white hair and distinctive, black eyebrows. But the eyebrows of Lubbers are historic. They're of Brezhnev proportions. Yet – between Lubbers and Leers – Lubbers is the one who is known for his leers. Bu-dum-bum. (These are not jokes I made at the event.)

The event was a meeting for the Society of Old Dutch Christian Democrats. That wasn't the official name, but that's how it felt. The place was crawling with them. The speakers included Ruud Lubbers, who was interesting. (Peter van Uhm, retired four-star general in the Royal Netherlands Army and former Chief of Defense, was excellent.) But the one I really wanted to hear didn't speak: former Immigration Minister Gerd Leers. His party CDA was in the coalition with Geert Wilders, and I was curious to know how much of the immigration policy was dictated by the PVV.

Next up, I performed my routine, comparing Dutch politics to US politics: 'In America our elections take 18 months. In the Netherlands there are some governments that don't even exist 18 months.' Part of me thought I might be asked to leave the building – or the country. But then I was approached by a man in black with a big, silver cross. He introduced himself as the Bishop of Maastricht, and he said he loved my speech. Before I knew it, he'd introduced me to Gerd Leers. And there I was, face to face with 'Mr. Immigration.'

Gerd Leers was charming and cordial. I paid him a compliment: 'It seems you're irreplaceable as Minister of Immigration. Because in the new Cabinet there's no more Minister of Immigration.' Leers explained that his portfolio had been taken over by the Ministry of Security and Justice. 'Of course!' I thought. I'd just read that the Justice Ministry had resolved an ongoing conflict by granting amnesty to child asylum-seekers and their families. I asked Mr. Leers, 'Did the Justice Ministry step on your toes by dealing with a problem that you were unable to solve?'

Leers said he was glad to see the issue resolved. But as Leers explained: 'There's a big downside. Make no mistake: if I could, I would grant amnesty to most asylum seekers. But at some point you must realize that – by giving everyone amnesty – you are giving a huge gift to the human traffickers.' He pointed out that over-generous immigration policies are sending the wrong message to immigrants.

As an example, he mentioned Bosnians in Germany. The German government began a policy of paying Bosnians to return to the Balkans. Anyone who'd been in Germany longer than two years would be paid thousands of euros to repatriate. The result – according to Leers – was that newly rich Bosnians were coming home and rebuilding their houses with German taxpayers' money. And worse – more Bosnians were now moving to Germany with the express purpose of staying for the minimum two years, just to grab the money and return home. Clearly, these people were gaming the system. But I couldn't help thinking, 'What would *I* do, when these wealthy Western nations hadn't done such a good job of protecting my home in the first place?'

We agreed no one likes human traffickers. It's a huge industry, shuttling the poorest people to the West with false promises, in appalling conditions. But – according to Leers' logic – those poor people should have the decency to stay put! Or they should all save up for a ticket on KLM and arrive like civilized people.

*

Back to 'The Year in Politics.' The event was held at The 'Royal Foyer' of the Amsterdam Stadsschouwburg. In attendance were members of the new right-wing Dutch Cabinet. And even Hero Brinkman. I'd prepared quite a bit of material about the new Dutch government, but I hadn't expected them to be standing there ... I thought of Stephen Colbert, took a deep breath, and went into it:

'You've got to give Geert Wilders and the PVV some credit. Like Hero Brinkman says, someone has to do something about all this anti-social disrespect for Western values, like ...

- ✔ The guy who head-butts someone at a bar and puts him in the hospital.
- ✔ Or the guy who commits sexual misconduct in the workplace.
- ✔ Or the guy who beats up his girlfriend, while the girlfriend is pregnant.

And of course we're not talking about immigrants. We're talking about the PVV:

- ✔ Marcial Hernandes (head-butt).
- ✔ Eric Lucassen (sexual misconduct).
- ✔ Dion Graus (domestic abuse).

'These are not just *supporters* of the PVV. They ARE the PVV. They're elected members of Parliament, who represent us. Every time the PVV gets in trouble is another reminder that the *allochtonen* aren't so bad. Where does Wilders find these people? There's also the guy who had to step down because of financial impropriety. And the guy who got caught sending inappropriate tweets. And don't forget the guy who got drunk and went on a rampage in the Parliamentary press club!'

Ouch. With that last line, I was making direct reference to Hero Brinkman himself. To his credit, Brinkman made no secret about his alcoholic outburst, and he's since been drink-free. I found myself at the bar after my standup set, and there was Brinkman. How would he react? He smiled at me, gave me his Free Drink vouchers and said 'I won't be needing these.' Well played, Brinkman. Well played.

I should have quit while I was ahead. Standing next to Hero Brinkman was Fred Teeven of the 'law & order' VVD Party – and State Secretary for the Justice Ministry. Here's the material I did about him and his party:

'Most cabinets have four legs. A Dutch cabinet mostly has three legs. This Cabinet has two-and-a-half… It's kind of wobbly. How did this happen? Well, as we immigrants are taught, Nederland is a democracy. There are elections, and the most popular parties get the chance to form a coalition. Right? The three most popular parties were VVD, Labor PvdA and PVV. So shouldn't they form a coalition? NO! In the Netherlands, democracy is not just a 'popularity contest!' There has to be an *informateur*. The KEY to Dutch democracy is one, unelected guy, who takes his favorite parties behind closed doors and *then* tells you what the *actual* coalition will be.

'*Informateurs* are appointed according to one qualification: NO PERSONAL INTEREST in the outcome of the Cabinet. One of the *informateurs* was Uri Rosenthal, of the VVD Party. As it turns out, he's now a member of the Cabinet. But I'm sure that was just a coincidence. The real architect of the coalition – the one who made sure the #2 biggest party would NOT be represented – was Ivo Opstelten. And now he's now Minister of Justice… Sorry, they changed the name. Now it's: Minister of *Security* and Justice. Like in America: Security first, Justice later.

'Is it me, or does this Cabinet seem crooked? I'm from Chicago, and I know crooked politicians when I see them. The Rutte Cabinet? I call it "The Ikea Cabinet." It looks nice at first, but you know it's never going to last a whole four years.'

I avoided Fred Teeven after that. But I did see Hero Brinkman again. He quoted Fred Teeven as saying, 'I hope this kid doesn't come to me to extend his residence permit.'

Thank goodness, I already have a passport.

Town of Lies

'Welcome to the town of Lies – Population 800 million!'

CHAPTER 10

Pain Tolerance

All the criminals and drug addicts in Europe have gone and exploited the openness in Amsterdam. ...Amsterdam is a mess.

– The O'Reilly Factor, *Fox News*

Dutch doctors prescribe the least amount of antibiotics in Europe.

– *De Volkskrant*

In America, we're pretty sure that all Dutch people are drug-dealing, drug-doing, baby-killing, grandpa-murdering homosexuals. Yet – if that was true – then you could get drugs from, say, the Dutch health care system, which is virtually impossible.

My grandpa used to watch *Fox News*. He'd call us up and ask, 'Are you doing okay over there?' As if to say, 'How do you manage to survive?' I'd tell him to relax and watch that YouTube video *Fox News vs Amsterdam*. It does an excellent job of listing drug abuse, murder and suicide as American problems, more than Dutch.

And then my grandpa would go further: 'But I hear you've got socialized medicine over there. You can't even see a doctor, if you want to.' And that's when I'd have to set the record straight: 'Seeing a doctor here is not a problem!'

...The problem is getting the doctor to do anything.

Most countries have doctors swear an oath: some version of the Hippocratic oath. In Nederland, there seems to be a different oath: 'As much as possible, I will tell my patients "Why don't you go home and get some rest?"'

It is not uncommon to begin and end your doctor visit like this:
'I have a head cold.'
'Why don't you go get some rest?'

'I have a chest cold'
'Why don't you go get some rest?'

'I have a head cold, and because I was waiting so long in your waiting room, now I also have a chest cold. Also, I'm suffering from acute depression since no one is taking me seriously. And my arm was bitten off by a squid, I'm losing a lot of blood.'
'...Why don't you go get some rest?'

The frustrating thing for an American is this: the advice is absolutely correct. For me, staying home from work and healing myself has worked every time. (And imagine if I'd have a job that paid me for sick days!) But – as an American – I want the option to pump myself full of antibiotics and keep on working. My wife continues to tease me about it.

My wife has such an antipathy to drugs she gave birth to two babies with nothing but deep breathing. My family in America still doesn't believe it:
'But when did you have the epidural?'
We didn't.
'But what kind of anesthesia did you use?'
Nothing.
'... Are you doing okay over there?'

Granted, we could have gone for a hospital birth if we'd wanted it. When my wife opted for natural childbirth, that was one of my first questions. Refreshingly, the midwife assured me she was not anti-drug; she was just pro-nature. We were told: 'If there's anything wrong at any point, that's when we go to the hospital.'

We did end up going to the hospital at one point, which convinced me not to trust the hospital. About a month before the due date of our first child, my wife got a strange feeling. Normally, she'd be feeling the baby move or kick every day. But there were a couple of days in a row that she felt nothing. As a first-time mother, she got super-nervous. So, on a Sunday, we decided to go in to the hospital.

If I can recommend a day of the week to go to a Dutch hospital, I would not recommend a Sunday. Even if my wife had been giving birth, I think they would have asked, 'Can you hold it in until tomorrow?' We were told that there was only one obstetrician on duty, and there was another woman in labor, so we'd have to wait. I explained that my wife was super-nervous, and we just needed a consultation. Just someone in a uniform to tell us everything was okay. We waited.

While the obstetrician was busy, we were visited by an obstetrician-in-training. She showed us into a room, and we explained again that we were super-nervous. She made an ultrasound scan of the baby and paused as she held the wand over my wife's belly. Then we got the famous Dutch bedside manner: 'Either I'm reading this wrong, or your baby has birth defects. It could be a misshapen head. I'll go get the doctor now (and be gone for as long as possible).' We were scared stiff.

She literally left me holding the ultrasound wand in my hand. I decided to keep smiling. I thought I'd make the best of it: 'What the hell, I'll give myself an ultrasound.' I introduced my wife to my food baby. That helped us calm down a little, but it felt like forever before the proper obstetrician came in. Without a word to us, he instructed the trainee that you're supposed to measure from the outside of the line, not the inside. He left – still without a word to us. The trainee said, 'Your baby's fine.'

And I felt much better about having the baby at home.

Then the day came. The water broke. At this point in the story, my family wanted to know: 'How did you get to the hospital?'
We didn't.
'But who delivered the baby?'
The midwife came to us.
'In an ambulance?'
No, in an old Volvo.
'... Are you doing okay over there?'

To tell the truth, we were supposed to go to the hospital. When the water broke it wasn't totally clean, and that means you're supposed to have breathing machines nearby, just in case. I watched as the midwife called the hospital and was told there was no space. Why? It was a Saturday.

The midwife continued dialing. My wife continued dilating. The midwife found another hospital. Again, no space. Finally, she found an open spot at Slotervaart Hospital – the same one that said maybe the baby was deformed. But my wife had already dilated to eight centimeters.

The midwife and I looked at each other and silently did the math. To an American, eight centimeters doesn't sound so big. But multiply that times the three flights of stairs we'd have to descend to get to the street. And then what? I couldn't believe there was no plan for this. We could call an ambulance. Or maybe it would be faster with her Volvo? Or a taxi? I actually thought a taxi might want to take us. For the record, according to the List of Least Desirable Passengers, 'Pregnant Woman' is right up there between 'Vomiting Vagrant' and 'Bleeding Junkie.'

In my desperation, I even thought of our normal mode of transport – the bike. Of course, I didn't expect she'd ride herself! But part of me seriously considered taking my wife on the back of my bike. I somehow pictured the midwife biking along beside us, yelling, 'Pull your knees up! Keep breathing!' And if worse came to worst and a scooter would try to pass us, I'd hijack it.

As it turned out, we didn't make it out of the bedroom. We had our first baby on our bed. No anesthetic, no defects, no complications.

And then – as directed – we went and got some rest.

Our second baby was an even more touchy-feely experience. The water broke and again the amniotic fluid wasn't clear. And this time it was a Monday. Surely we could get to a hospital this time? Not even close. Everything went much faster. This time, we used what is called a 'birthing stool,' which allows your baby to be born with the help of gravity. So instead of 'Push, push!' our midwife had to say 'Hold it in!'

Our second midwife's name was *Door* – a uniquely perfect name in either language. As the baby was crowning, she was busy with some special pillow. My wife remembers it as one of our pillows with a garbage bag around it. Door was getting ready to catch the baby as it fell, naturally, out of the womb. She and her assistant were in the room, but they weren't ready yet. I was standing behind my wife, who was doing her best to slow things down, but at one point gravity took over. My wife said, 'I can't hold it anymore!' I could only watch as Door grabbed the pillow and made a diving catch! She went all out. I can still see her diving, in slow motion. And Door – not my baby – hit the floor.

What followed was a kind of shamanistic gore-fest. The midwife's assistant stepped in and made a whole production out of the afterbirth. With bravado, she said, 'Wait, there's more!' and proceeded to do an imitation of the magician pulling handkerchiefs out of the sleeve. She pulled until she reached the placenta, but no one was there to catch that. The placenta hit the floor, and the blood sprayed all over the walls like a special effect in a horror movie.

The midwife's assistant then gingerly picked up the placenta and cradled it in her arms. It was like a little competition. Midwife Door was with our baby, saying, 'Ooh! It's a boy, he's beautiful!' And next to her was the assistant, looking at the placenta, saying 'Ooh! Look at these beautiful textures! Did you know the placenta weighs as much as the baby? You made this. You did this! *Kijk, die mooie vliezen. Mooie moederkoek.*'

Yes, the Dutch word for placenta is 'mother cookie.' I've made my peace with terms like 'shame hair,' but 'mother cookie' was a bit much for me. I couldn't help thinking, 'How could you invent such a term? Was there someone long ago who was ready for a post-birth snack?' And – right on cue – the assistant asked, 'Do you want to keep it?'

My wife and I both stared at her for ten full seconds, before I volunteered, 'What?'

The assistant explained, '*De moederkoek*. Some people like to keep it.'

I wanted to know why. Are there really people who eat it? Is it a Dutch thing I don't know about? Maybe I don't want to know...

But my wife was looking at me over her shoulder, saying, 'I don't know. Maybe we'll want it. We can plant a tree with it...'

As I watched my newborn being neglected, it occurred to me, 'Let's not have this discussion now.' Sometimes, just give the people what they want. I told the assistant, 'Fine! Wrap it up. We'll take it.'

For months afterward, if you'd come to our house and drop in for dinner, we'd be ready. We'd just have to look in the freezer for fishsticks, pizza, or if you ever wanted to try some 'Mother Cookie...'

*

To this day, I have never managed to get myself antibiotics from a Dutch doctor. Although, we came close with my daughter one time. She was just a few years old, and she had an ear infection.

We took her to our doctor, who told us, 'Why don't you go get some rest?'

We protested, 'No one is getting any rest! Our daughter is screaming in pain. Her mama is not sleeping. I'm not sleeping. We need some medicine.' We were recommended some over-the-counter cream. It was at that point that we decided to try alternative medicine – the homeopathic doctor.

The new doctor started out with another typical Dutch doctor phrase: 'What do you think is the problem?'
Like it's a medicine quiz.
'We think our daughter has an ear infection.'
The doctor said, 'You are right.'
I half-expected to win a prize.

Then came the next question: 'And what would you like me to do?'
I've heard this question more than once from Dutch doctors: 'What do you think I should do?' It's not the best way to inspire confidence. My first reaction is always, 'You're the doctor. Don't *you* know?'

But, looking at it another way, if a doctor asks 'What do you think I should do?', seeking your opinion like you're some medical expert, it really is quite a compliment.

I summoned up the manner of a doctor who'd been studying pediatrics for years, and I offered my advice. 'We'd like some medicine!'

The doctor quickly determined the root of the problem: an outer ear infection on her right side and an inner ear infection on the left side. We were given two prescriptions. Both had magically illegible scribbles, and we looked on in awe as the woman at the pharmacy actually seemed to understand what they meant. But we were taken aback when she delivered the medicine: chamomile oil and *zuurdruppels*. We thought this might be a mistake... But no, the woman explained that the chamomile oil was for the outer ear infection and the sour drops were for the inner ear. At home, we wrestled our poor child into position and administered the chamomile oil first. In with the cotton ball. And then the flip over and the sour vinegar drops into the other ear.

It was then that it occurred to my wife: 'We're mixing oil and vinegar in our daughter's head.' And she wasn't getting healthier very quickly. But when she sneezed, the salad dressing tasted great.

The Netherlands is a country where you can get smart drugs over the counter, no problem. And (with a weed pass), you can get hash over the counter, no problem.

But if you want to get antibiotic medicine to heal your body, Dutch people say 'Get out of here, you sick, disgusting freak.'

Noliko
Potatoes your kids won't like.

CHAPTER 11

SINT'S LITTLE HELPER

You're only here because you're black.
– Johan Cruyff to Edgar Davids

As a comedian, I love Zwarte Piet. Black Pete is good for business. Santa Claus has his elves; Sinterklaas has his *negers*. Some people say Zwarte Piet is racist, such as the group of people who protested the annual Sinterklaas parade with T-shirts saying '*Zwarte Piet is Racisme*.' Of course, the cops arrested them. ... Otherwise people might have noticed.

I remember a science fiction film, where the aliens emit a substance that makes humans thinks they're adorable, instead of hideous. Zwarte Piet seems to emit a similar substance that works specifically on Dutch people.

For years, I've been performing shows at Boom Chicago Comedy Theater, making jokes about Zwarte Piet. The most entertaining bit is always after the show, when Dutch people passionately argue that Zwarte Piet is not really black. They insist: 'It's the soot from the chimney' that gives Zwarte Piet his red lips, hoop earrings and afro.

I was invited to sit on a panel to discuss Zwarte Piet, and I said *yes*. The event was called 'Zwart van Roet' (black from soot). The panel was hosted by Quinsy Gario, the founder of 'Zwarte Piet is Racisme.' He's also the one who was arrested – and beaten – for wearing his T-shirt at that Sinterklaas parade. Was he bitter? A little.

I decided to share my story about Zwarte Piet. It's the same story I tell in the Zwarte Piet show at Boom Chicago. My kids are half-Dutch, and they love Zwarte Piet, But it got awkward when he came to our door.

My wife is Dutch, and – according to her – we celebrate Sinterklaas in the 'traditional Dutch way.' That is to say, we do it as simply as possible. We get a sack full of presents and we give it to the neighbor. The neighbor waits five minutes and drops the sack at our door. He rings the doorbell and runs away. The kids then open the door and – even though there's no one there – they scream and cheer with glee. It's the most cost-efficient theatrical trick ever devised. No costumes, no actors, just a sack of props and a huge result. Leave it to the Dutch.

One year, when my daughter was three, we finished dinner early and got ready for presents and *pakjesavond*. It was almost 6 o'clock, it was already dark, and – before my wife could say 'Zwarte Piet will be here soon,' we heard the doorbell ring. My wife looked at me to ask, 'Did you go to the neighbor already?' I shook my head no. But my daughter – being three years old – was already at the door. She yelled 'Yay!' and whipped open the door. And there, standing in the doorway, was a guy with a black face, dark curly hair and a brightly colored red & yellow outfit. The outfit said 'DHL Post.'

Now I don't know whose decision it was to send this guy out delivering packages on the 5th of December. But sure enough, my daughter was living the dream, her eyes filled with joy. I was looking at her, thinking, 'Please, don't say it…' and moved towards her, but not quickly enough! She raised her hand and yelled, 'Zwarte Piet!'

My wife and I were frozen, as the color drained from my face. Our eyes locked as we got whiter, and the DHL guy got redder. The American in me was paralyzed with shame: we've made my daughter a racist!' But the Dutch part of me just said to play along: 'That's right! It IS Zwarte Piet! Sometimes Papa has to sign Zwarte Piet's Magic Clipboard! And Papa hopes Zwarte Piet never has to take the 5 December evening shift again.'

*

Consistently, after I tell that story onstage, I'll have someone come up and ask if I made it up. 'It's not true, right? The part about your daughter pointing to a black person as Zwarte Piet?' How could it not be true? It happens all the time.

At the 'Zwart van Roet' event, there were plenty of black Dutch people with the same story. One man said he was in a café in late November, when he found himself being laughed at. There was a four-year-old Dutch kid who'd called him Zwarte Piet. The man responded by telling the parents that people should know the difference: 'No hat, no feather, no Piet!' They just laughed at him.

Another man had a kid point at him on the street and call him Zwarte Piet. He told the kid 'I'm not buying presents for you.' The man said the parents were so offended they wrote a letter to the newspaper claiming *they* had been victimized: 'With that kind of attitude, this man is just asking for trouble.'

I've received similar feedback from telling my story online. Here are some examples:

- ✔ 'These complainers are just hyper-correct white people or aggrieved descendants of slavery who look for a reason to complain. They're just the latest batch of moochers who would rather complain about nothing than do something with their lives.'
- ✔ 'Every year, you people feel discriminated because of a little black makeup? Show a little character.'
- ✔ 'Non-white people who complain should start their own tradition of dressing up in sandals and long hair because they're all doing one big hippie imitation.'

And those were *nice* ones. Then there were these:

- ✔ 'Shapiro, it's simple. Follow our traditions or get out.'
- ✔ 'To be honest, you sound like a twat. merry christmas numb nuts.'

(Note: these comments were given anonymously or pseudonymously.) (Note: they are reprinted with misspellings intact.) (Note: the misspellings are not as bad as the comments left by some native speakers, so you can give them some credit.)

Further feedback highlights American holiday hypocrisy:

✔ 'We'll eliminate Sinterklaas, when you give up fat Santa.'

✔ 'How can Americans lecture us about Sinterklaas with their over-commercial Santa Claus? It's like the Vatican lecturing us about child abuse.'

✔ 'Santa Claus is helped by elves who are very small people. Is this not equally discriminatory?'

I've received so many comments that center on Santa's elves that I feel I should point out a key distinction: an elf is modeled on a mythical creature. Zwarte Piet is not. For the comparison to hold true, the American tradition of Santa's helpers would have to be some kind of ethnic Dutch stereotype. For that logic to hold up, Dutch people would have to be living in America and confronted at Christmastime with a character called, say, 'Buck-Tooth Dutchie.'

Santa would always be accompanied by a bunch of Americans dressed up like Anky van Grunsven and dancing like horses. It may not be very flattering. Nor very accurate. And – when Dutch people would complain – the Americans would respond, 'Don't be silly! We love all you square-faced, square-toothed Dutch people. Now dance like a horse for us!'

The Zwarte Piet issue became clearer when Geert Wilders pulled out of the Dutch cabinet in 2012. There was a big headline in *Spits,* saying: 'ZWARTE PIET VOOR WILDERS.'

To me, 'Zwarte Piet for Widlers' could only mean one thing: 'Zwarte Piet Supports Wilders Politically.' This seemed unlikely.

BUCK-TOOTH DUTCHIE

Or 'ZWARTE PIET VOOR WILDERS' could also mean a 'Zwarte Piet is being given to Wilders,' perhaps as a personal assistant. Then the black-face would offset the hair dye.

Or perhaps it was *voor* in the sense of *before*. As in 'We'd work with Zwarte Piet before we'd work with Wilders.' That was closer to the truth. But also totally wrong.

I had to ask a Dutch friend of mine to explain it to me:
'It's obvious! "ZWARTE PIET VOOR WILDERS" means Wilders is taking the blame for crashing the Cabinet.'

Me: 'Okay. But why *Zwarte Piet?*'

Dutch guy: 'It's from the card game, when you end up with the Joker. That's the Zwarte Piet.'

Me: 'So Zwarte Piet is The Joker? That would be an interesting Batman remake…'

Dutch guy: 'No, Zwarte Piet means you take the blame, you lose. You get the Zwarte Piet.'

Me: 'Ah. And of course Zwarte Piet isn't really black – he's just painted black. So "Wilders Is Being Painted Black." Like *zwartmaken*?'

Dutch guy: 'Yes! *Zwartmaken* is bad, Wilders is bad.'

Me: 'So Zwarte Piet is bad – ?'

Dutch guy: 'NO! Zwarte Piet is good!'

Me: 'But if *zwartmaken* is bad then making someone black is bad…'

Dutch guy: 'Well, Zwarte Piet isn't really black. It's just the soot from the chimney!'

Me: 'Okay! So what's the bad part? The soot is bad?'

Dutch guy: 'No.'

Me: 'Okay! Then the black face is bad?'

Dutch guy: 'No.'

Me: 'Okay! Then just BEING black is bad.'

Dutch guy: 'Yeah... but in a good way.'

*

Back to the 'Zwart van Roet' event. The guy behind the 'Zwarte Piet is Racisme' T-shirts is Quinsy Gario. A highlight of the Great Zwarte Piet debate was Quinsy sitting next to Jeroen, the director of the kids' show *Sinterklaas Journaal*. You've got to give Jeroen some credit for showing up. He started by giving a compliment: 'Intelligent debate so far. I admit, I'd assumed you'd all be just a bunch of "Bijlmer types."' (The Bijlmer area is renown for its high concentration of African and Caribbean citizens.)

Good old Dutch honesty. And, thus, whatever credit he'd had was immediately thrown out the window.

Jeroen of *Sinterklaas Journaal* went on to insist that Dutch people do not see Zwarte Piet as black. He insisted: 'It's just the soot from the chimney.'

I wished for his sake that he'd have brought his lawyer along: 'Jeroen, did you not see the poster for the event? Did you not read the title?'

Further, Jeroen denied that the makeup for Zwarte Piet is called '*Neger Zwart*.' While they debated that point, we watched as the technician did a Google search on the big screen onstage. Again, Jeroen insisted: 'It's not called "*Neger Zwart*".' And on-screen we were looking at several examples of makeup called '*Neger Zwart*.'

By the end, Jeroen admitted that maybe the depiction of Zwarte Piet could be seen as offensive to 'certain' people. He admitted that next year they should do things differently: they should write in a few lines about how Zwarte Piet is not really black.

I watched this year's *Sinterklaas Journaal*. I didn't see anything about how Zwarte Piet is not really black.

Yet, I also noticed that my daughter grew out of her phase. She no longer confuses black people with Zwarte Piet. In fact, when she was watching the (white) actor Eric van Muiswinkel on TV, she recognized him as the Head Zwarte Piet, even without the makeup.

To be honest, my kids are now old enough to no longer believe in Zwarte Piet, and to no longer want to celebrate Sinterklaas.

What's to become of Zwarte Piet? At the 'Zwart van Roet' event, there was an organizer who told how he went around to all the shops on the Bijlmerplein and lobbied them to remove Zwarte Piet imagery from their windows. I couldn't help thinking: 'Why waste your time with Hema shop windows? The Hema headquarters is right around the corner at Bijlmerplein 355!'

It was by appealing to the management of Dutch confectioner Buys that they agreed to change the name of their traditional cookies '*Neger Zoenen.*' (*Zoenen* means kisses.) (*Neger* you can guess.) After some pressure, the name of the chocolate covered marshmallow cookies was changed to simply '*Zoenen.*' No shame, no blame. Just change the name.

Quinsy Gario ended his comments demanding that all Dutch people admit that Zwarte Piet is racism. I don't see that happening. But I do see some signs of change. McDonalds had a whole ad campaign for a dessert with *pepernoten* – the traditional cookies thrown by Zwarte Piet. The ad featured a nighttime Amsterdam skyline, blanketed in snow. That was it. No Sinterklaas, no Zwarte Piet. It still got the point across.

But personally I hope Zwarte Piet won't disappear. He really is great for the comedy business.

Black Kids for sale
Can't get enough of that slavery.

CHAPTER 12

Acting Dutch

Do we need a translation into Dutch? Nah…
– My publisher

Since I abruptly truncated my American acting career to move to the Netherlands, I was happy to find acting work here. If there's ever a Dutch production needing an English-speaking character, I'll sometimes get the call. And sometimes I'll get the call for an American who can speak some Dutch. But – in my experience – does anyone really want that?

I've played a casting director on *Onderweg naar Morgen*, a catty modeling coach in *Radeloos*, and a news reader in *Phileine Zegt Sorry*. One of my favorite gigs was for the soap opera *Goede Tijden Slechte Tijden*. In one of the story lines, the young love interest goes on a ski holiday and injures herself. Who plays the doctor? Me.

When I got to the set for *GTST*, I said, 'It's an American doctor, right?'

'No. He has to be French,' was the answer.

'But the lines are in English.'

'Well, just say them with a French accent,' they said.

And there I was on the set with Barbara and her daughter Charlie (Charlotte Besijn and Aukje van Ginneken). We were running our lines, and I wasn't sounding French enough. I tried a thicker accent. Again the director asked, 'More French, please.' Just for fun, I did a crazy, broad French accent – somewhere between John Cleese in *Holy Grail* and Inspector Clouseau. I was expecting the feedback to be negative. But the director didn't say anything, so that's what I did for camera. If you ever watch the clip back, you might be able to hear everyone on the set dying with laughter in the middle of the scene. Based on the normal production level of *Goede Tijden, Slechte Tijden*, I considered it an improvement.

And then someone thought it would be a good idea to have me on the Big Film Quiz *De Avond van de Grote Film Quiz*. Every year, Dutch Public Broadcasting gets a bunch of Dutch actors and makes them compete in a number of challenges involving film trivia. Sometimes they have to identify film quotes, and sometimes they compete to do the best re-enactment of famous film scenes. And every year it's pretty fun. The host is Matthijs van Nieuwkerk from *De Wereld Draait Door* – the closest thing the Dutch have to *The Daily Show*.

I know Matthijs van Nieuwkerk from his days as director of Amsterdam broadcaster AT5. It was there that we did the *Boom Chicago News* in 2001. I know he speaks English, but he's made a rule for himself not to do it on TV. According to a former producer on the show, he once did an interview with an American actor – the guy who played Ridge on *The Bold and the Beautiful*. Apparently the plan was for Matthijs to treat the guy like an intellectual and ask him their trademark difficult questions, in English. Unfortunately, Matthijs didn't feel 100% comfortable in English, and the plan backfired. Since then, he's made it a rule: 'Only in my native language.'

... If only I had followed that rule.

The Big Film Quiz was on Dutch Public Broadcasting. The producer asked me if I could speak Dutch on the show. I asked why, and the explanation was: 'Unlike commercial television, the public broadcasters are aimed at, shall we say, *higher*-educated viewers.'

As I understand it, English-language programming is associated with 'lowbrow' programming, like Derek Ogilvie talking to dead people or Paul Turner on *Expeditie Robinson* – both on commercial TV. Then there's the American, Dan Karaty, on *So You Think You Can Dance*. And they do live shows, where subtitles are a challenge. (It's always entertaining when they do try. Karaty will say something like 'Nice technique, but I wanted to see more performance, more expression, more attitude, more wow, more swagger!' ... and the subtitle will come up a few seconds later: '*Goed, maar het kan beter.*')

Yes, commercial TV uses a lot of English. Yet, when Dutch people watch these shows, they are in fact processing two languages. Pretty smart for 'lower-educated' viewers, I'd say. In fact, why are the 'higher-educated' viewers watching public channels not trusted to be multilingual?

*

In 2012, Pep Rosenfeld and I came close to being on *Pauw en Witteman*. Boom Chicago was asked to develop material for the 2012 election. Would we be willing to spend a bunch of hours developing and trying out material linking the Dutch election to the US election? Yes. And would we be willing to come in and try it out in the studio so the producers and Jeroen & Paul could see? Yes. Was it funny? 'It was very funny,' they explained. 'It's just ... we want to wait until Leon de Winter is on the show. Then we'll invite you.' We watched as Winter came and went. We're still waiting.

To their credit, many producers in Dutch public broadcasting have had no problem putting me and my English on TV. On BNRfm I did an Obama column with Bas van Werven, and we did it with questions in Dutch and answers in English. I spoke English for NOS *Election Night* in 2000 with Boom Chicago. I was with Pep Rosenfeld on *Twee voor Twaalf* in 2008. And in 2004 – the same night that Theo van Gogh was murdered – we were in Hilversum for US election coverage on *Barend en Van Dorp*. That was one of the most surreal experiences of my life. One dressing room was filled with Dutch politicians and commentators in shock; the other was filled with the obligatory popcorn and brownies and American football cheerleaders waving pom-poms.

Pep Rosenfeld and I once went on *Lingo*. As a promo for Max Westerman's show *Westerman's Nieuwe Wereld*, we were invited to play the classic Dutch anagram game versus Westerman and Kay van de Linde. Granted, Pep and I were mixing Dutch with English; a joke. We didn't come close to winning. But at least it proved Americans could play the game. For a long time, no one thought Americans would be smart enough to keep up.

I was once part of a pilot project to prove Americans could play *Lingo*. They brought over the classic US game show host Chuck

Woolery. While we were waiting for him to arrive, they had us wave our goodbyes in advance: 'Bye!' We went over the rules: five-letter words. No proper nouns. And then we started the game. My partner and I sailed through Round 1 and made it to the final. But then we got tripped up on a J-word. Time ran out. Chuck Woolery said, 'Ooh, I'm sorry. The answer you were looking for is *Jesus*.' For a moment I looked confused, and then I blurted out 'That's a proper noun!' Even if you don't believe in Jesus, you still have to capitalize the name. But then I realized why they'd taped our goodbyes in advance. The final cut is Woolery saying '*Jesus*' – I look confused. Then it cuts to us waving 'Bye!'

In 2012, I did my solo series *Verkiespijn* in English on VARA *HumorTV*. It was subtitled, with a mix of English and Dutch. I interviewed comedian Horace Cohen, who has American citizenship.

I asked him, 'Are you going to vote in November?'

Horace said, 'Yes! Definitely. At the Embassy on Museumplein, right?'

'Technically, that's the Consulate,' I said. 'And no, you can't vote there. You have to request an absentee ballot and send it in.'

Horace replied, 'Oh, well then no, I'm not going to vote.'

We agreed Obama could use a more motivational slogan.

Horace suggested 'Voting Made Easy.'

Or if we're being honest: 'Vote Obama, unless it's too much trouble.'

It was rather complicated wordplay: a little bit of English, a little bit of Dutch. No problem.

I've come close to being interviewed on *De Wereld Draait Door*. The producer explained that they were getting complaints about having the same guests all the time. And in 2012, they wanted some people talking about America who were actually from America. A week before they were going to have me on, they tried some new faces at the table. Then they were getting complaints about too many guests they'd never heard of. So I got bumped for Leon de Winter.

I teased the producer from *De Wereld Draait Door,* saying, 'I hear the public broadcasters have a secret "No English" policy.'

She said, 'It's not just English. It's any other language.'

'A-ha!' I said. 'So there is a policy?'

She explained: 'There's no written rule that Dutch public broadcasters have to stick to Dutch. But there's an unspoken rule that – if you're accepting money from the Dutch government – then you're expected to stick to the mother tongue.'

Thus, Dutch broadcasting acts as a sort of *'Academie Nederlandaise'*. While the Dutch don't like to think of themselves as chauvinistic, they can give the French a run for their money.

I suppose that's why I quite enjoyed it when Matthijs van Nieuwkerk invited guest-host Adriaan van Dis to take over the show for Book Week. Adriaan van Dis came on, and the first thing he did was switch language. First came a fluent German interview, and then a fluent English interview. Three languages for the price of... well, less than Matthijs van Nieuwkerk. That was a pretty good deal.

*

So back to *The Big Film Quiz*. The producer wanted me to play the character of a Hollywood reporter, in Dutch. I asked if it might be a bit more believable if I could speak mostly English, with a little bit of Dutch thrown in. He said *yes*.

Here's the script they gave me.

"*Mijn naam is* Greg Shapiro from The Hollywood Reporter *en ik ben* delighted to be invited at the *Avond van de Grote Filmquiz. We verwachten hier* anytime *de limousines met de sterren van de avond, de acteurs en actrices. Het zijn kopstukken van de Nederlandse film en televisie, die het lef hebben om zich hier vanavond te onderwerpen aan een spervuur van vragen. (kijkt achterom)*

En hier is Georgina Verbaan …"

Just a little bit of Dutch.

I was hoping they wouldn't mind if I threw a bit more English in there.

The concept was not only for me to introduce the show. I was also to provide a through-line to the wacky ending. Every year on *The Big Film Quiz,* they end the show with something unique. One year it was a *Full Monty* tribute where all the guys did a striptease. This year the plan was an ode to the classic American Pie Fight. The plan was that I would get steadily drunker on champagne during the show. And then – when they'd bring out the big birthday cake, I'd say something naughty and get hit in the face with cake.

Here's what really happened. First of all, I did the intro in broken Dutch. I said hello to Thomas Acda, Daniël Boissevain, Frank Lammers, 'the Meisjes [girls] van Toren C,' and Johnny de Mol. They walked from the limo to the theater – and walked all over me. In the studio, I was given an earpiece, which I always hate. The words in your ear never match the situation on the ground.

The earpiece: 'Keep getting drunk! We need to see you drinking!'
The director: 'What are you doing in the shot? Shapiro, stop moving.'

You can watch the clip on YouTube. For most of the show, they didn't have me in frame. So at the end of the show – with no explanation at all – a drunken Shapiro came onscreen. Out of nowhere I staggered into frame with enormous cakes. It was spectacularly awkward.

The earpiece: 'Shapiro! Go Shapiro.'
The director: 'What are you doing?! Wait for Matthijs!'

I delivered the prizes, I presented the cakes, I waited for Matthijs.

The earpiece: 'Start the Shapiro speech!'
The director: 'What Shapiro speech?'

They told me to write up a little speech and make it so insulting the actors would really want to hit me with cake. In practice, all I got out was '*Jullie Nederlanders zijn ZO bezig met elkaar …*' And then Thomas Acda and sore loser Frank Lammers ignored me and started throwing cake at each other.

Here's the text I'd prepared: 'You Dutch people are SO busy with yourselves. Dutch film festival, Golden Calf award, Edison award, Rembrandt award … "Let's give each other more awards!" But meanwhile you don't have any Dutch films on the show tonight. All you talk about are American movies. All your clips are in English. Yet you make ME speak Dutch? You've all got your heads up your asses!'

As it turns out, maybe it's best I got hit in the face when I did.

As the host of the show, Matthijs van Nieuwkerk knew what was coming, and he made it clear to us he did not want to be hit with any cake. It was Frank Lammers who walked over and put cake directly into Matthijs's hair. In the YouTube clip, you can see a slightly chagrined Matthijs van Nieuwkerk, covered in cake and signing off 'We hope to see you next year...'

There would not be a next year.

Scamm
Come in and get scammed.

CHAPTER 13

Dutch Meetings are from Mars

For most cultures, a decision is the end of the discussion. For the Dutch it's the beginning.
– V. Bekker, NiNsee Institute

Dutch office culture is, to me, based on paradox. How can a meeting start out so much like an American meeting, but then end so differently?

Dutch meetings and American meetings both start by getting to the point. Other meetings start quite differently. I've had the pleasure of attending meetings in a few different cultures. As an amateur cultural anthropologist, I've noticed that business meetings are a bit like foreplay. In that sense, Dutch meetings are from Mars; Belgian meetings are from Venus.

In Belgium – even Flanders – I've found that the culture is more inspired by the French. Belgian meetings are more like foreplay for women.

Yes, your meeting starts with coffee, but it's nice coffee. Espresso coffee. You drink your coffee at a café table, where you can watch your coffee being made, just for you. A conference room? *Non!* No one's thinking about that right now. Tell me, what would you like with your coffee? Perhaps a cookie? Not just a cookie, but a nice cookie. Nothing you have to unwrap – these were made fresh, just for you. And you look like you might enjoy some of our fine chocolate as well. Perhaps there's a menu for the fine selection of fine chocolates to go with your fine coffee, just for you. Take your time, what's the rush? How was your journey? How are you feeling? What's on your mind? Business, you say? *Oui, oui*! Let me take you to my conference room…

Dutch meetings are like foreplay for men. 'Here's some coffee. Let's get to business! Business! Business! (Cheese sandwich.) Business! Ahh… That was good business. Want a cigarette? The smoking area is outside. *Doei*!'

To me, coming from New York, the Dutch way feels more familiar. Yes, Americans will ask 'How are you?' But they don't really care. For fun, you can honestly tell them how you're feeling and watch as the Americans react, dumbfounded. Like the Dutch, the Americans tend to get to business.

Unlike the Dutch, the Americans expect an agreement to end the meeting. Dutch meetings seem to exist as an excuse to have more meetings. American meetings will sometimes end with 'let's agree to disagree.' Dutch meetings are more like 'let's disagree to agree.'

This brings me back to the seminar 'Dutch Identity: Who Are We?' There was a speaker who'd done a survey of Dutch managers. He asked the Dutch 'What's the most important factor for your Job Satisfaction?' He'd offered choices such as: Salary, Recognition, Opportunity for Promotion, Daily Commute, Travel, Perks, Lease Car. But according to the survey, most Dutch didn't pick any of those. The most important factor for them was Autonomy. Self-determination. Freedom. Apparently, this trend goes all the way back to the revolt against the Spanish occupation; the Dutch don't like people telling them what to do.

There are definitely benefits to the Dutch management style. While many cultures have 'top-down management,' the Dutch are more innovative.

I was working on a project, doing 'explain-imation' for a Dutch innovation: water-cooled Ultra-Low Temperature Freezers. Standard freezer design involves removing heat from the freezer and blowing it into the air. A Dutch engineering team looked at the design and thought, 'Why not instead remove the heat with water? The freezer effectively becomes a water heater.' The design would cut down costs and help the environment. The result? No go. Why? The Dutch engineers were working for a Japanese company. According to the Dutch team, their Japanese bosses clearly valued R&D… but only when the top management asked for it. Eventually, they took their idea to a competitor. Don't be surprised if you see it at Philips.

The downside of the non-hierarchical Dutch management style is that hard decisions can be hard to come by. Put another way, the Dutch change their minds so much it's a miracle anything gets done.

Once, I was hired to perform some tailored standup at a corporate event for a product launch. At least that's what I thought. Because that's what they told me. But I should have known better.

To prepare for the product launch, I was invited to a meeting. The woman who'd hired me introduced me to her colleagues. And as she reviewed what I was supposed to do, they all took turns second-guessing the plan, until it was time to go, and we weren't sure of anything anymore. That's when I got to witness a Dutch tradition: 'I know what we said at the meeting, but at the meeting to review the meeting, we decided we should do it completely differently. So, when can we have a new meeting, and another meeting to review the meeting about this meeting?'

Why did we need so many meetings? It was explained to me: '*Iedereen moet z'n plasje er over doen.*' Literally: 'so everyone gets a chance to piss on your idea.' There's such an emphasis on consensus. Everyone should agree on everything. Yet – far from being agreeable – many Dutch meetings I've attended feature the most negative, contrary, cynical conversations I've ever had.

I've been to Dutch meetings where everyone agrees on a proposal so quickly it makes them uncomfortable. You can tell the Dutch managers are feeling: 'This can't be right!' And then someone says '*Ja, maar…*' 'Yes, but – what if… ?' It's like every Dutch manager grows up with an inner insurance salesman – a little built-in Actuary to calculate every possible risk:

'Yes, but what if he's not funny?'

‘Yes, but what if our audience has no sense of humor?’

‘Yes, but what if there’s someone in the audience who’s having an affair with someone else in the audience and he makes a joke about inter-office affairs and they are offended?’ (actual quote)

Back to the product launch. The woman who’d hired me called me back and invited me to a follow-up meeting. Only this time – instead of being hired – I was back to ‘Maybe Hired.’ I made myself available for a conference call. That turned out to be a bad call. Literally. It was a bad connection with distortion any time two people spoke at once. Especially disturbing was the fact that they were a telecommunications company.

I once heard a saying ‘A camel is a horse, designed by a committee.’ That’s what they were attempting in the conference call. They’d sent me a briefing with different people’s input in different colors. One wanted tailored standup. The other wanted live role-play. One wanted no more than 30 minutes. Another wanted no less than 45. In the conference call, I said ‘I’ve read your briefing, and I’m still unclear what you all want. Why don’t we start from the beginning?’ Bad move. There was no one person taking charge of the conversation. Again, I heard conflicting requests. They said they’d call back.

Afterward, I got an e-mail saying I’d lost the job. It was an angry e-mail, blaming me for a lack of professionalism. The e-mail was in fact a series of e-mails from everyone on the conference call.

Babette: ‘In the conference call, Mr. Shapiro asked us to start from the beginning. I couldn’t hear everything he said, but did he even read the briefing?’

Ingrid: 'I couldn't hear everything that was said, but Babette said that Mr. Shapiro said he didn't read the briefing.'

Monique: 'I couldn't hear everything. But Ingrid said that Babette said that Greg said he didn't even bother to read the briefing. We have chosen not to work with Mr. Shapiro – for obvious reasons.'

What's funny to me is that most of these women probably had a degree in Communication. I don't know if 'Chinese Whispers' was part of the curriculum, but it seems they learned that lesson very well. They also learned a valuable lesson from sending that e-mail: don't FWD me their e-mail addresses. Because – as an American – I'm not afraid to send a 'Reply All' telling them they're idiots.

I found out later that the client really wanted neither standup nor role-play, but a video.

At times like these, I guess I'm just glad I could help them figure out what they didn't want.

ADD Business Ctr.

'Let's do business. ... Hey! Shiny car!
I like bunnies.'

CHAPTER 14

Dutch Honesty + Dutch Courage

People always talk about the Jews in WWII. But the Germans, they were no angels either.
– Hans Teeuwen, *cabaretier*

Another paradox about the Dutch is their reputation for being tolerant, but also for telling people to '*doe normaal*.' Be normal. But the longer I live in the Netherlands, the more I realize what '*doe normaal*' really means. It really does mean you should be yourself. In fact, if you're too full of yourself or putting on airs, there's a kind of built-in Dutch bullshit detector that will kick in and cut you down to size.

Before living in the Netherlands, I spent most of my time living in Chicago and New York.

In Chicago, people focus on your past: 'You're from Missouri? I have a friend from Missouri. Wanna hang out?'

In New York, people focus on your future: 'You're from Missouri? I'm from Mississippi. Anyway, what's your plan to get rich and famous?'

Amsterdam is a mix of Chicago and New York: 'You want to be rich & famous? Cut the shit! Where are you from? Mississippi? Don't care! Plus, here's my favorite insult about Mississippi: you have sex with your sister! Why don't you laugh?'

I've had this conversation with Dutch people more than once: 'Hey, I saw you onstage! You are not very funny. Are you really from America? I thought so. You're so loud! And you don't know anything about the rest of the world. You look angry. Do you want to shoot me? You Americans, always shooting each other. Bang bang!'

When I meet Dutch people, it's often as if they want to show off some new Truth Serum they just drank. 'Your nose is big!' 'Your suit doesn't fit right.' 'You look Jewish!' And this was a quote aimed at a female colleague of mine: 'You looked really nice onstage tonight! I was looking at your trousers, and I'm pretty sure you shave your pubes. But my friend says you have a full bush. So which is it?'

In particular, Dutch honesty and Dutch courage can be a tricky combination. In the days following 9/11, I was here in Amsterdam. A couple times, after I'd do a show, there would be a Dutch guy who wanted to talk to me:

Him: 'Are you really American?'
Me: 'Yeah.'
Him: 'Terrible what happened in New York.'
Me: 'Yeah.'
Him: 'Let me buy you a drink.'
Me: 'Thanks.'
Him: '*Proost.* (sip) You know, you really did have it coming.'

Me: [Spitting my beer]
Him: 'Oh yeah… America had it coming. Who gave the Afghan rebels their weapons? Reagan. Who created the Saudi terrorists by propping up that oppressive regime? The Bush family.'

The problem was I agreed with the argument. But if I'd have said it, they'd have called me a terrorist.

In retrospect, I wish there had been more drunk Dutch guys in the Bush White House.

Some Dutch people have raised bluntness to an art form. You may have heard of Dutch comedian / *cabaretier* Hans Teeuwen. If possible, do not get in an argument with Hans Teeuwen. I learned this lesson the hard way.

It's hard to find anyone in the Netherlands who doesn't know at least one Hans Teeuwen quote. He is celebrated for his irreverent imagination ('Nostradamus in his tight green pants') and his embrace of taboo (miming wild sex with Queen Beatrix). In the UK, he's a cult phenomenon, known for his wild stage presence and gleeful politically incorrect material. Onstage and off, he is an advocate of free speech. And he practices what he preaches.

In 2011 I saw Hans Teeuwen perform live at the TEDx event in Amsterdam Stadsschouwburg. Luckily, I knew a bit about him, and I knew what to expect. Much of the crowd, however, had no idea what was coming. Hans Teeuwen at TEDx was rather like putting fireworks in a dirty diaper at a 'Let's Keep Clean' event.

Bear in mind, TEDx is a day-long conference with the theme 'Ideas Worth Spreading.' Many of the ideas were about how to make the world a better place. Teeuwen came on and started by mocking the entire event by covering Michael Jackson: 'Heal the World... Make it a Better Place... for you, and for me, and for THE ENTIRE HUMAN RACE!' He commented on sustainability by smoking a cigarette onstage and saying 'Wouldn't it be great if my cigarette could last forever?' And then he went to the piano. He did a parody of World Music: 'The worst kind of music in the world.' He described most World Music as 'a bunch of Africans chanting.' This moment was especially awkward because the act that was on right before him was an African choir. More awkward was that they had to come on again after he was done.

I had a chance to speak to Hans Teeuwen after the TEDx performance, to ask what he thought of it. He said he was just trying to make a point about the hypocrisy of some of these people, who talk about saving the planet, but are mostly just flogging their own website or book or product.

I asked him, 'Is that why you took the gig, to make a point about freedom of speech?' He replied, 'Nah, I just did it for the money.' To this day, I'm not sure if he was being ironic. Being American, I have to assume it was irony, and I just didn't get it.

The day after our conversation, I wrote about it in my blog. I included his quote 'Nah, I just did it for the money,' and I ended there. I thought I'd let the reader judge if he was being ironic or hypocritical.

Months later, Hans was developing a new solo show. I'd heard of a great open-mic space for try-outs, so I called him up about it. It was a Sunday, and he picked up right away. He didn't say much and let me talk. He continued to not say much...

And then he broke in, 'Wait a moment, Mr. Shapiro. Is this the same Mr. Shapiro I spoke to after TEDx?'

I said *yes*.

Hans continued, 'I mean the same Mr. Shapiro who was trashing me online?'

My jaw dropped. My testicles retracted. I don't know if it's possible to turn deep red through the phone, but I tried my best.

I had no idea Hans had read my blog! (Did anyone?) I found myself scrambling to remember what, exactly, I'd written. But he spelled it out for me: 'Oh, I know what you were doing, Shapiro. You were just trying to kiss up to the do-gooder crowd. You were trying to make friends with the organizers and kiss their sweet, sweet asses. You thought that by trashing me you could make a better name for yourself, Shapiro. Well, you didn't think I'd read that shit, did you? But I did! And now you're feeling pretty awkward, aren't you? *Aren't you?!*'

Clearly, Hans was enjoying himself. I could hear him smile as he spoke. He was on a roll. Even as I cringed in agony, I could tell I'd earned myself a custom-made mini-performance. It was like finding an insult comedian and pissing him off, just to hear him rant about you. But then there was silence. I was supposed to speak. Of course, I felt I had to apologize for causing any offense.

And then he went off again, 'Oh, that's easy, isn't it? Now that you have me on the line and you want something from me, now you apologize…' [technically, I was offering something to him] '… and how lame, really, Shapiro. You roll over just like that? "Sorry if I offended you." Do you stand by anything you say? Or do you just sell yourself out when it's convenient? Who's the one being hypocritical now?'

I concluded the conversation by again offering a tryout space if he needed it. He replied, 'No, I knew right away I don't need the space, thanks. I just wanted to make you feel shitty. Okay, bye!' Bravo.

And here I go again. Hans Teeuwen yelled at me for trashing him online, and now I am trashing him in a book. Have I learned nothing?! Part of me hopes I'll get another custom-made performance by Hans. But I sure hope I get to be the one with a drink in me next time.

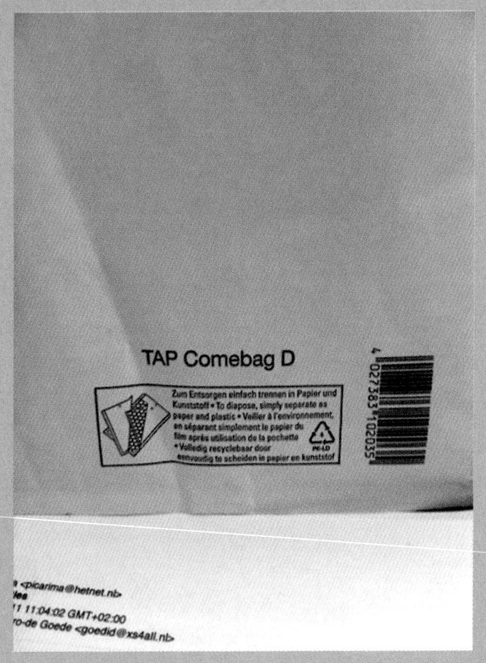

TAP Comebag D
Zum Entsorgen einfach trennen in Papier und Kunststoff • To dispose, simply separate as paper and plastic • Veiller à l'environnement, en séparant simplement le papier du film après utilisation de la pochette • Volledig recyclebaar door
te scheiden in papier en kunststof
PE-LD
4 027383 102035
<picarima@hetnet.nl>
11 11:04:02 GMT+02:00
ro-de Goede <goedid@xs4all.nl>

Tap Comebag

In the Netherlands, even the post envelopes are obscene.

CHAPTER 15

No Subsidy for You

We've become a nasty little right-wing country.
– Youp van 't Hek, columnist / *cabaretier*

The New York Times recently wrote that the Amsterdam arts scene is 'under siege.' And – as a member of the Amsterdam arts scene – I agree it's certainly had its ups and downs. Literally. In 2011, the Dutch government decided that – instead of only 6% sales tax for our services – it would be 19%, like everything else. And then, after six months or so, they dropped it down again. Why did they raise it in the first place? The new right-wing government apparently wanted to make a statement about the arts. If the statement was 'we have no idea what we're doing' – they succeeded.

I also noticed the statement they made by declaring what would be exempt from the tax hike: the cinema. Apparently, 'normal' Dutch people don't need whiny high-art; they just want to go to the movies. In practice, they mostly go to American movies. Effectively, the tax exemption was a subsidy for Hollywood. On behalf of Hollywood, thank you! That's just what we needed.

As it happens, the *New York Times* article was written by Nina Siegal, who was my former editor at the former *Time Out Amsterdam*. She explained to me how she took a maternity leave and was subsequently laid off. I asked, 'Isn't that illegal?' Yes, it is. Apparently the magazine also wanted to make a statement: that they are reckless bastards. I told her that – at times like these – it's important to look on the bright side. Specifically: *Time Out Amsterdam* is now bankrupt, and Nina is writing for *The New York Times*.

Nina's article for *The New York Times* focused less on the random tax policy changes and more on the other, more permanent bit of arts reform: slashing subsidies. These are changes that aren't limited to Amsterdam. At issue was the Theater Institute Nederland, whose funding was completely cut, and now they're closing down. Over the years, they've amassed a fairly large representation of Dutch theater history, which is now being sold off. If only the subsidy had been slashed by 90%, they could have at least kept the lights on. But no – 100% cut. The article also mentioned Dansgroep Amsterdam. And I've watched the same thing happen to the Dutch Slavery Institute NiNsee, as well as Amsterdam's Theater Engelenbak.

And here we get to the quote from above. Youp van 't Hek is one of Nederland's foremost *cabaretiers*. (*Cabaretier* is the Dutch name for ' better than comedian.') (Though these days many *cabaretiers* are trying to be more like comedians.)

Remember Buckler beer? No one does. Buckler was a non-alcoholic beer, which was around before I got here. The story goes that Buckler was shamed into pulling their product from the Dutch shelves, thanks to one man who kept ridiculing them, mercilessly. His name: Youp van 't Hek. His last name is hard to pronounce, but it sounds a lot like 'Fanatic.' And he fanatically hated Buckler beer.

It's nice to think that a comedian can affect social change. (But where is he now that Bavaria 0.0% is assaulting the airwaves?) More importantly – as civic legend has it – Youp van 't Hek used his influence to save the Kleine Komedie Theater from closing down. But even Youp could not save Theater Engelenbak.

To be fair, Youp did join a number of artists in a group effort to save Theater Engelenbak. 'We all started in Engelenbak' was the ad campaign. And a lot of well-known artists did start there. Engelenbak got a lot of sympathy. There was an attempt to get them some sponsoring from the private sector. But in the end, they shut down, putting the blame firmly on the shoulders of the Amsterdam city council. I even contacted the organizer of their famous open podium 'Open Bak' and offered a space for them to continue. 'No,' was the answer. 'We're still busy trying to tie up all the loose ends the city left us ...' I guess I can't blame them for being bitter. And maybe they'll eventually join the entrepreneurial spirit spreading through other areas of the arts scene.

Is the arts scene in Amsterdam in fact under siege? In many ways, yes. But that doesn't have to mean it's dead. In my neighborhood, there are pop-up ateliers and galleries growing in new, unused spaces. Yes, the big money is being thrown at the big projects: Stedelijk, Van Gogh, and Rijksmuseum. But I'm seeing artists rejecting the handouts and setting up shop in squats. Forget the crumbs; freedom's in the slums. In fact, it reminds me of the arts scene when I first encountered it in the '90s.

When I was performing in Chicago, I knew only a few people who were getting a subsidy. But there was no shortage of theaters. Chicago is known for its 'storefront' theaters, where unused retail space becomes performing space. One of my favorite theaters is even located above a funeral home. In America, there's a perpetual arts funding crisis. But there's something to the phrase, 'Hey gang, let's put on a show!' Meanwhile, the phrase, 'Hey gang, let's write a subsidy proposal and wait' is less well known. The downside is clear: you often end up working for free. Or – as I like to call it – 'investing my time.' And sometimes the investment pays off.

In 2009 I was hosting a jazz series in Amsterdam, sponsored by Arrow Jazz FM. At one point we learned our funding was being cut, because Arrow Jazz was going off the air. Somehow I came up with the idea: 'Why not organize a benefit concert to "Save Arrow Jazz FM?"' We were doing the jazz series at Sugar Factory in Amsterdam, and they gave their permission to set up an event. (It probably helped that my father in-law is one of the owners.) Since the cause was Arrow Jazz, it proved refreshingly easy to get people to donate their time. We had Hans Dulfer and his band. We had Wicked Jazz Sounds. We had Benjamin Herman from New Cool Collective. And my favorite was Zuco 103 with Brazilian sounds from Ms Lilian Vieira herself. Did we succeed in keeping Arrow Jazz on the air? No. Did I make any money doing it? No. But I'd generated good faith with some musicians. And when Caro Emerald sold out three nights at Amsterdam's Heineken Music Hall, and the band needed someone jazzy to introduce her... I got the gig. I like to think my investment paid off.

Admittedly, some investments haven't paid off yet. I'm still not getting paid for my Dutch news vlog. But I'm still doing it.

Ever since *Comedy Central News* went off the air, people kept asking me: 'When are you going to make Dutch news videos again?' At one point I thought, 'Why not do it on my own? Maybe I could get a subsidy!' I'd applied for a subsidy once, and I'd learned a lot. Specifically that I never want to apply for another subsidy. So I tried a few other ideas.

- ✔ I did a daily vlog for XM News, but they went bankrupt.
- ✔ I made a pilot for nu.nl, but they were reorganizing.
- ✔ I made a pilot for AT5, but then they had their subsidy crisis.

So now I'm making *Behind Dutch Headlines* for free and hoping the sponsors will find me.

Luckily, I found a Dutch guy with the same idea, who's just as crazy as I am. If we ever get paid, so much the better. If not, then at least we spent our time creating and not waiting.

Given my background, I find it odd that a theater would rather die than go on living without a subsidy. In fact, since I've never had a subsidy to create a show, I find the whole attitude rather insulting. It feels rather like they're making a statement: 'Any show one would make without a subsidy (like mine) is a show that's not worth making.' Perhaps true creativity can only be unlocked with adequate funding. But if you want to see real creativity, try existing without funding.

I came to Amsterdam to work with Boom Chicago Comedy Theater. I've been told by many Dutch people it's crass and commercial. Yes, it would be nice to perform to an audience that's not ordering drinks during the show. But then there wouldn't be a theater for very long. Since I've started touring my solo shows through Nederland, I even built an intermission into my program, so the theaters can make a profit at the bar. I was surprised to find that half the theaters are still serving the drinks for free.

Sometimes I tell my fellow *artistes* about the early days at Boom Chicago, and their mouths fall open. We had to do on-street promotion for every show we performed. That was the rule: three hours of promo for every two hours of show. We were meant to go after the tourists. Specifically the English-speaking tourists. I learned pretty quickly how to spot them from a block away. *Invita* backpacks and tight-fitting clothes? Italian. Sporty, outdoor mountain-climbing gear and baggy jeans? Those were the Americans. Stag parties staggering in the gutter? Those were the Brits.

On-street promo was like music lessons. I hated to get started, but I was always happier once I got into it. It was basically just asking people 'Where are you from?' and being interested when they'd answer. Eventually, they'd respond, 'What are you doing over here?'

'Well, since you ask, I happen to be doing a comedy show…'

In Edinburgh at the Fringe Festival, we even had tickets with us to sell on the spot. The line for the Fringe ticket office was long, and most people had one thing in common: they were overwhelmed by the sheer amount of shows. I'd state my bias as an uninformed Yank, but then I'd offer reviews on what I'd seen so far – and what I'd heard about the options in the show guide. 'What are you up for? This show? I saw it, overrated. That show? I was drinking with them, and they're lovely. My show? Right here…'

At one point in my promo back in Amsterdam, I used a secret weapon: bounce shoes. My boss had bought them, thinking they'd help with jumping. But the real advantage was: speed. Part of the problem of on-street promo is timing. Sometimes you wait and wait for the right people, but when they show up, you're not positioned well. With the bounce shoes, I had a much bigger range. I could run 50 meters in about five seconds. Sometimes I'd make eye contact with people across the Leidseplein and they'd think they were safe from awkward physical contact. But then – boing! boing! boing! – I'd be handing them a flyer. It even helped selling tickets to the shows, until the shoes broke.

If I'd have had a choice, I probably wouldn't have picked on-street promo. I'd much sooner have chosen 'Get Subsidy & Hire Promo.' But – in retrospect – I'm glad for all that experience. It was on-street promo that was my introduction to Dutch actor Peter Faber. My colleague Rob was doing on-street promo when he met Matthew Broderick and Sarah Jessica Parker, in line at the Anne Frank Museum. Another colleague was promoting when he met Burt Reynolds, who ended up visiting Boom Chicago and coming onstage to steal the show: 'Is this my real hair? Yes. Because I paid $5,000 for it.'

*

One of the guests we had at Political PARTY was then-Minister of Culture Ronald Plasterk. It was fun teasing him about subsidies. Pep Rosenfeld asked Plasterk 'Why has the Minister of Culture never been to see Boom Chicago before? It's because we're in English, so we don't really count, right?' Minister Plasterk diplomatically responded that he is very happy with the commercial success of Boom Chicago. In fact, Plasterk even continued by mocking the way Pep sneaks self-advertisement into his shows: '… and by the way, I hear Boom Chicago has a very special Valentine's Day show coming up!'

Sticking to his guns, Pep followed up a little later, 'Minister Plasterk, can you help Boom Chicago get a subsidy?' Plasterk laughed and said, reassuringly, 'You don't need a subsidy. Everybody wants to see your show already.'

Pep responded, 'So… your job is to give money to shows that people *don't* want to see?' Plasterk tried to laugh it off, but there seemed to be at least a kernel of truth, as he begrudgingly nodded '*Ja*.'

Juncker Bike

When you want a bike that will last, try the 'Junker'.

CHAPTER 16

The Open Street is Closed

Then, from behind, a bicycle slammed into me...I turned and saw a young, brunette cyclist in a short skirt. She looked awfully cute. She also looked mighty pissed – at me. She scowled, then muttered "*Klootzak!*" and sped off. – Pete Jordan, author 'De Fietsrepubliek'

I bike. Even in Chicago I used to bike. If ever you've seen the one madman, biking in the middle of a snowstorm, it may have been me. When I came to the Netherlands and saw the standard means of transport, a part of me felt like I was home.

My first bike in Nederland was a rental. Then I had a loaner. I asked where to get my own bike, and – at least in Amsterdam – the common answer I got was 'Go find a junkie.' One night I was accompanying a friend of mine home, when – sure enough – a junkie approached us and said, '*Fiets te koop*.' This meant 'Wanna buy a bike?' My friend offered 50 guilders, and presto he had a bike. The next night, I found myself wandering the same street on the way home, with 50 guilders in my pocket.

It was near the Red Light District that I found a thoroughly disreputable-looking gentleman on a bike, saying 'Wanna buy?' I nodded *yes* and followed him around the corner into one of the myriad shadowy corners. I looked at the bike. It seemed rather new. I asked, 'How much?' And he said, '25 guilders.' This seemed a bit too good to be true. All my instincts were now telling me I was in over my head. If I'd been brought up in New York City, I'd have said 'I don't like this,' and walked away. But I'm from the Midwest, and I felt that it wouldn't have been polite.

I held up 25 guilders and asked 'Can I try it first?' Now nervous, the man said 'Yeah. Here,' and he gave me the bag he was holding, so he could turn the bike around. To my surprise, he hopped on the bike and took off – with my 25 guilders. Like an idiot, I followed him, saying 'You forgot your bag...'

A quick examination of the plastic baggie proved that I hadn't purchased a bike at all, but instead what looked like crack cocaine. It's possible I'd purchased crack. More likely was I'd encountered an Amsterdam tradition: fake drug dealers. It's one of the more enduring scams in the city. And it's not technically illegal, since no one was in possession of any real drugs. It's just some powder made to look like a rock of crack in a baggie.

At this point I'd drawn a bit of attention to myself, since I was holding up a bag of drugs in the street. Even in Amsterdam this can draw attention. One downtrodden guy was looking at me curiously. I said, 'Can you believe it? I was trying to buy the bike. Instead, I got fake drugs.' Wide-eyed, the guy said 'Let me see that...' The way he cherished the bag, I'd started to think maybe it wasn't fake. It occurred to me to say 'That'll be 25 guilders,

Sir…' But in retrospect, I was happy to get out of there with my syringe virginity.

The junkie bike. At one point, everyone I knew had one. My boss even had one, covered in red and yellow tape. Decorative. That's how I learned a valuable lesson about Amsterdam biking etiquette. My colleague had borrowed the fancy, taped-up bike from our boss. Together, we were riding side by side in the bike lane. At one point, the bike lane merged a bit with the sidewalk, and two pedestrians started shouting at us in Dutch. We weren't sure what we'd done wrong, but one of these guys had lunged at my colleague and started grabbing the bike. It soon became apparent that this pedestrian was – in fact – the one who'd meticulously applied the red and yellow tape, since it was his bike. And he had every reason to believe we'd actively stolen it. My colleague was trying to explain: 'I didn't steal the bike! I'm just borrowing the bike. From the guy who paid the guy who stole your bike…' And after realizing what he'd just said, he immediately gave the bike back. I gave him a lift home.

Now we had to explain to our boss what had happened to his bike. He just laughed 'Easy come, easy go. Sorry to put you in that situation.' That would not be the last awkward situation. Another colleague of mine was caught on camera. On the front page of *Het Parool*. They were doing an exposé on the rampant sale of junkie bikes in Amsterdam, and they had a tryptic of photos chronicling the sale, with the faces blurred. But to anyone who knew him, it was obvious: that man was our colleague 'Peter G.' The location was right next to Boom Chicago. Of course, Boom Chicago was not implicated.

I like to think I've paid for my junkie bike sins, in that I've had so many of my own bikes stolen over the years. Although I guess I can't really call it stealing when I leave my keys in the lock, like an idiot.

*

There's something indeed very Dutch about bike path logic. Everything functions fine, as long as you know your place. Dutch bicyclists will tolerate a lot, but if pedestrians like Pete Jordan wander into the bike path, it's *tring tring!* and *klootzak*. I find it charming that Amsterdam bicyclists can be so optimistic. Surely they must notice that the streets are full of tourists, some times of year more than others? Surely they'd anticipate the increased likelihood of a collision based on the season? Nope. All too often, the bike bells ring as if they're genuinely surprised that some group of tourists is impeding their progress.

While biking in the Netherlands, it is never okay to judge people on the basis of color. Unless they're riding a group of matching-colored bicycles. Then you can be sure they are tourists on rental bikes, who are way more dangerous than when they're on foot. They're possibly high, and they probably don't know how to bike. Just the other day, I was almost run over by a group of matching green bikes. They were all blithely biking through a red light, as if assuming 'green bikes mean green lights.'

Now, you might expect me to go off on a rant about scooters here. But I'm not falling into that trap. Scooters are a real litmus test to see just how tolerant you are. I'll admit I've flirted with road rage when scooters have raced past me on the bike path.

I even yelled at a guy one time: 'You're supposed to ride in the street!' He actually stopped and explained the rule: blue number plates mean you can ride on the bike path; yellow means you're supposed to ride in the street. I suppose I was happy that there was a well thought-out system. Never mind that – when he'd passed me – there were three yellow number plates stuck in traffic, and his blue number plate was whipping past me so fast I'd still felt my teeth rattling.

I realize a lot of blue plate scooters are modifying their engines and breaking the rules – which is why I was so thrilled to see the police stop the kid who'd raced past me. But mostly I have no problem sharing the bike path with scooters. Clearly, there are worse things. Specifically, the things that block the path entirely. Sometimes, these can be the Double-Wide Chat Rooms: people biking next to each other so engrossed in conversation they become unaware anyone might want to pass them. Even if I'm biking next to someone, I don't mind if I hear a scooter *toot-toot* from behind. In fact, anytime I'm biking 'double wide,' I'm half listening for the *toot-toot* – sometimes so much so that my Dutch conversation partner complains that I'm not giving her my full attention. (Sorry, dear.) Yes, the Netherlands is a crowded place, and you must be very spatially aware. Unless there's a really good chat going on.

It's handy to know the rules of the road. Of course, I know the basics from studying for my American driver's license. But that was nothing compared to the Dutch driving exam. As well as the Practical exam, I was required to take the 'Theory' exam. ('Why does driving exist?') In the Theory exam, I got to properly learn all the rules I thought I knew. But many I'd learned incorrectly.

For example, when leaving a roundabout, it's important to signal clearly – even for bicycles. From biking in the Netherlands, I'd learned from example: yes, you should signal, but not too overtly, as that would be uncool. From experience, I knew the appropriate way to signal was to look as if you're handicapped and can barely raise your arm.

There are, of course, downsides to knowing the rules of the road. I was once doing a gig for a corporate event, leading a walking tour through Amsterdam city center for a bunch of international investors. They'd been to Amsterdam before. I just had to be entertaining, while taking them from Hotel Grand to a *jenever* bar and a boat tour. I had my clipboard, and I was ready to go. But then we came to some road construction.

It's hard not to encounter road construction in the Netherlands. Indeed, the Dutch term for 'Road Closed' is '*de straat is open,*' literally 'the street is open.' Dutch football guru Johan Cruyff once famously said 'Every disadvantage has its advantage.' Johan Cruyff is perhaps also the guru of Dutch road construction: 'A street is only open when it is closed.'

Dutch people like ripping up the streets so much I think sometimes they do it just for fun. Sometimes a street will be perfect for two weeks, and then it will be ripped up again for no apparent reason. Perhaps it's just to make work for people. I call them the Brick Flippers. I've watched as they pull the bricks up from one side of the road and replace them on the other side. This is the code of the Brick Flippers: 'Some bricks have been face down for two weeks! We must flip them to the other side. We have to be fair to both sides of the brick.'

So there I was with my tour group of investors. The already narrow street was made even narrower by the road construction. They looked at me with trepidation, but I guided them through as confidently as possible. And then – hallelujah – we came to the zebra crossing.

I stood in the zebra crossing and beckoned my group to cross. There were a couple Spaniards who were clearly nervous about the whole thing. And sure enough, as I was standing there in the crosswalk, I heard the angry ringing of a bike bell coming at me at full speed. I'd expected to see tourists, but it was an older Dutchman. All I could do was swat at him with my clipboard as he whipped by me.

I got everyone safely across the bike path, and I realized the Dutchman was right behind me. He was swearing at me in Dutch and English: 'You don't have to hit me, *hè*? I am going my own gang, *hè*? You don't hit people with your clipboard! *Je wil met me vechten, hè*? You want to fight?'

Clearly, I could have said sorry and moved on. But I couldn't help it. I said: 'I just took the Dutch driving exam, and it's very clear: all wheeled traffic must stop when pedestrians are present in a crosswalk. And by the way, I'm leading a tour of your city and trying to give these people a nice first impression. Right now you are that impression.'

I don't know why I thought that would work. Somehow I guess I expected that he would say 'Gosh. You're right. Thank you.' But instead we all got to learn the word '*Mesjokke!*' as he spat at me and took off.

*

I love it that in Amsterdam you use your bike for everything. You see moms riding bike with a rack on the front holding one kid; a baby on the handlebars. Two kids on the back and a third one standing on top of them for a play date. The family car in Amsterdam is a bike. No helmets. '*Doe normaal!*'

All this I've seen, it's normal. But what I saw for the first time in front of my house I still can't believe. It was the dad riding the bike, the kids on the front, and on the back was the mom, holding a little baby, who couldn't have been more than six months old. Then she took her hand off the papa, so she was just balancing on her butt. And she pulled up her shirt and started breast-feeding.

That is the true meaning of multi-tasking. That is the true meaning of freedom. That is the moment I knew I had truly arrived.

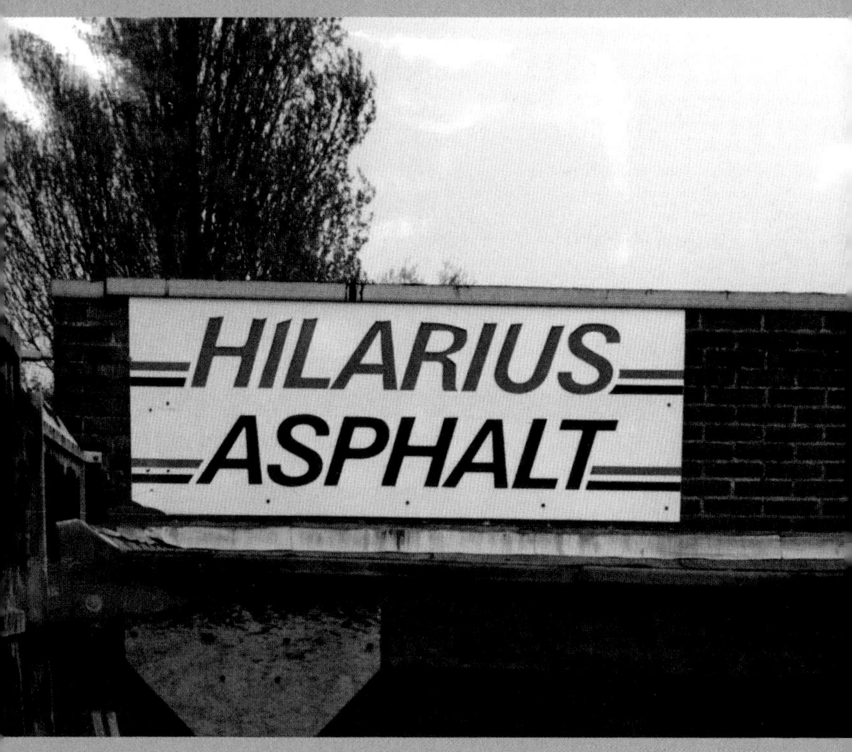

Hilarius Asfalt
Dutch road surfacing is extremely entertaining.

CHAPTER 17

Overcrowding, Overpaying

Wie parkeert, betaalt.
– Cition ad campaign

Good news, Planet! I'm sharing a car. Bad news: we're now playing a game called 'How many times over can you pay to park your car?' So far, the answer is: 5.

Nederland is indeed a densely populated country. Living in most Dutch cities is like living in Manhattan: a car is largely a liability, as parking is expensive. But since my father-in-law lives in our building, we decided to try car-sharing. That is, we told him; 'We're sharing your car.' Simple! With my wife and kids, we find ourselves using the car once every two weeks on average. My father-in-law uses it even less. When the time came to buy a new car, we thought 'Why not do it together?'

Since I use the car for work, we decided to put the car in my name. Again, it seemed like the appropriate thing to do. We got the car home and felt like celebrating… until we remembered the parking permit! It was still registered with the old car.

In America, I think I'd have kept the same license plates and physically placed them onto the new car. Here, that's not the case. To switch the old parking permit to the new car we'd have to visit the service center for the Cition Parking Company. Until then, we'd have to pay an hourly rate to park, just like everyone else. In our neighborhood, it's about three euros / hour, collected by the Cition Parking Company.

Number of times we were paying for the car now: 2.

Luckily, my parking app has no problem accepting a new license number. I use Parkline. We had no problem, until…

Problem A: Cition Service Center says you can't switch the parking permit to another owner. Even if you're sharing the car. There is apparently some logic to this plan. But all I understand is that I'm now paying an hourly rate to park the new car, while we're still paying a monthly rate to park the old car that's now somewhere in North Holland. We talked to the supervisor. Surely, this kind of thing has happened before? Surely, they're not discouraging us from removing a car from the overcrowded neighborhood? Surely they're not punishing us for doing the right thing?

Oh, but the punishment had only begun.
Problem B: It turned out my father-in-law had *also* turned on his parking app: ParkMobiel.

Number of times we were paying for the car now: 3.

You may know Cition Parking Services from their recent ad campaign, '*Wie parkeert, betaalt*.' 'If you park, you pay.' Their job is to collect revenue for the city. But apparently business is so good they actually have enough money left over for an outdoor advertising campaign, just to restate the obvious. I'm also in the business of buying 'ad routes,' and I happen to know that they cost thousands of euros a week.

Cition had been hired by the city to enforce the parking rules. But – as they love to point out – they don't make the rules. That would be the *stadsdeel* and the City Council. Just as we were considering an appeal to the city, a new outdoor ad campaign popped up, from the *stadsdeel* and the City Council. The campaign was all about keeping our neighborhoods greener and creating more space for walking and biking – by removing cars. We checked back with the supervisor at Cition: had the policy changed to help us promote car-sharing? Not yet. But – again – the outdoor ad campaign looked fabulous.

I have a friend on the Amsterdam City Council, and I asked his counsel. His advice was this: 'Good luck! I've tried to tell the registry I moved, but they keep sending post to my old address.'

It turns out the easiest solution was to change the ownership of the car back to my father-in-law, negating half the reason for getting a new car in the first place. And while we were waiting for the paperwork to go through, we noticed a jolly little conference of Cition agents partying around our car. They were abuzz with chatter about how many parking tickets they could put on the windshield before the schlemiel of an owner would notice. I joined my father-in-law in running over to the parking party to protest: 'We're already paying three times over!' But no…

Problem C: Parking apps only work if you've typed in the correct license number. It seems your smart phone is only as smart as you were frustrated when you typed in the details. My father-in-law had typed in the wrong license number. We had three parking fines.

The number of times we were paying for the car now: 4.

To review, we were paying:
- Monthly for a car we no longer own.
- Hourly from the right phone.
- Hourly from the wrong phone.
- 3x parking fines.
+ Hourly for a car with one-letter difference from ours – making: 5. Wherever you are, KLV 92 X, you're welcome.

And congratulations to Cition for all your extra revenue. Will they reinvest the money in improving their common-sense infrastructure? Nah. But hopefully they can afford a nice new redundant ad campaign soon.

B.S. builders

Call for a free bullshit estimate.

CHAPTER 18

Dutch Housing and Full Frontal Nudity

The Netherlands is one of the most densely populated countries in the world.
– Assimilation course

The Netherlands is the 24th most densely populated country in the world.
– Wikipedia

My first apartment in Amsterdam was brand new. It got worse from there.

HOUSE 1

When I first moved to the Netherlands, I had the idea that the whole country was a run-down, dystopian Sodom and Gomorrah. But my first-ever Dutch place was '90s *nieuwbouw* – functional Dutch luxury I'd never experienced before. Boom Chicago had arranged the place for a group of us. Spacious bedrooms, spacious kitchen. Teeny, tiny stairs. The building was on the east side of Amsterdam, by the Entrepotdok and the Scheepvaartmuseum. It was not what I'd call a charming neighborhood, but we had a view over the Oostenburgergracht from our living room. It was in that living room that we watched Nelson Mandela being elected president of South Africa on TV.

Apparently, the place had been bought by a Dutch couple. They'd wanted to move in when they got married. But something went wrong at the last minute, and they'd needed renters, quick. That's where we came in. For us it was great – the whole place was fully furnished. Everything was brand new. And – when we went to open the kitchen cabinets – we noticed that the dinner plates were still in festive wrapping paper saying 'Congratulations to the happy couple!'

At one point, we had to deliver our rent to the former bride-to-be. She was a tall, blond doctor. Apparently he was a doctor, too. Cautiously, we asked what had happened. She told us he'd had a 'fear of commitment' and backed out of the whole relationship. And then we got a long and spirited rant, introducing us to her theory that – as women have become liberated – Dutch men have become 'cotton balls,' *watjes*.

Dutch relationships. Sometimes they giveth. Sometimes they taketh away. A few years later, I was living in a place my roommate had found. We were subletting from a woman who'd moved in with her boyfriend. It was a nice place, fully furnished, and it was all going well… until one night there was the woman, crying in our living room. 'We broke up,' she explained. 'He threw me out!' We tried to console her 'Aww… there, there.' And around midnight, still sniffling, she looked up at us and said 'So – where are you guys going to stay tonight?'

HOUSE 2

In the second place Boom Chicago arranged, there was an even bigger group of us. This was right behind the Victorieplein in the Rivierenbuurt district. We'd heard Rivierenbuurt was a pretty quiet neighborhood, and this spot was perhaps the quietest. The five of us had the whole house to ourselves. The stairs were even narrower. My room, in fact, was accessed by a ladder. The south-facing balconies looked out to the lush, green courtyard, and as soon as we got in there, we flung open the doors and cranked up The Eurythmics. It was perhaps 15 seconds before the angry banging began. It was not the last time the neighbors would protest at us Loud Americans.

Our second place was the first time I'd encountered a phenomenon I'd never heard of before: the Rent Police. One day there was a knock on the door. My roommate opened it and announced the police wanted to come in. I assumed it was due to the neighbors complaining about the noise. But no, said the Rent Police, they wanted to check the details of our rental agreement. That sounded even worse. They asked how many of us were living in the place, how many were allowed to live there, and how much we were each paying. I said I'd feel more comfortable answering these questions if our bosses were present. They were the ones who'd arranged the rental. The Rent Police then explained the reason they were there: to protect us from our bosses. That's what the Rent Police are all about: not kicking people out, but making sure people are not being made to pay too much. What a concept. I felt more at home than ever.

Our second place was famous. Anne Frank had lived on our street. The Merwedeplein was where the Frank family lived before they went into hiding. As a sort of testament to her memory, there was an old synagogue around the corner, which was of course abandoned. At first, we thought of it as a chilling reminder what had happened to the Jewish population of Amsterdam. But after a while, we realized that there are still plenty of Jews in Rivierenbuurt. It's just that – like most religion adherents in Amsterdam – they'd rather be dead than seen in a place of worship. I believe the former synagogue is now an auction house. Literally, there are moneylenders in the temple.

And our second place was the first time I had to live with The Shelf. Dutch people are well known for treating sex as a natural part of life. Less well known is that they have the same attitude toward the toilet. I come from a country where going to the toilet is known as 'going to the bathroom.' The Dutch have no such linguistic confusion. In fact – in our house – they'd gone to the trouble of separating out the bath and putting the toilet in its own, separate room. This was so we could learn to say 'I'm going to the toilet' – and so that the process of pooping could be made unavoidably, distractingly pungent. Our toilet chamber was designed to be as tiny as possible. Frequently, my knees would knock the birthday calendar from the door. The exhaust fan was a lovely antique, possibly on the world heritage list, since it was clearly impossible to update or renovate it in any way. It was a callback to an earlier time, when exhaust fans were scheduled to revolve based on the lunar calendar. Once a month, you might hear a small *Erp*.

And then, of course, there was the famous Dutch inspection shelf. As I've read, it was designed as a shelf to inspect one's poop. When Freud invented the term anal-retentive, it is well possible he was referring to a Dutch patient. Whereas the rest of the world finds such a practice scatological and repulsive, the Dutch seem keen to pride themselves on what they've accomplished.

Granted, the inspection shelf is not as common, these days. But the Dutch still do make them. Recently, I went on a trip to a home improvement center, and there they were on display. I had to check if maybe they were old models that someone was trying to get rid of. But no, they were new. Clearly there's still a demand for the Dutch poop pedestal.

The reason we needed a replacement toilet was that – in our current house – we still have an inspection shelf toilet. Our house is like many old, Dutch houses built on sand: it leans over to one side. Thus, our toilet 'shelf' had become a toilet 'slope,' angled backward. Or – if you will – it's a like toilet 'stunt ramp.' Every time we flush, it's an adventure: will our brown heroes make it over the edge into freedom?

We still haven't replaced the toilet. Partly because I'll miss the excitement. Americans have been accused of being loud and arrogant, as summed up in the phrase 'They think their shit don't stink.' This may be largely true. But at least the shit is submerged in water.

HOUSE 3

My third apartment in Amsterdam was a short-stay. For a few weeks, I lived right in Amsterdam center – on the Nieuwendijk, by the Singel. It was a 17th-century building, straight from the Golden Age. And it hadn't been properly fixed up since then. Trying to feel at home in that tiny space was like trying to atone for some previous sins. Specifically, the sins of being too loud the year before. That apartment was the noisiest place I've ever experienced. I had no problem hearing everyone in the building having sex.

On Queen's Day it was so loud outside, the walls were vibrating. Not in a good way. I'd woken up hung over from the Queen's Night party the night before, and I soon realized I was in the epicenter of Ground Zero of the noisequake – right in between a stack of speakers blaring house beats and a concert stage they'd set up for Dutch *schlager* music. It was not a good match. For anyone who's ever considered being hung over and then remixing the awful, saccharine Dutch *smartlappen* with poorly syncopated house beats, I don't recommend it. Luckily, it was Queen's Day, so I left the house and continued drinking.

I moved out the next day.

I know someone who happened to arrive in the Netherlands at the end of April, and her first experience with the Dutch was Queen's Day in Amsterdam. She said: 'I was like "Is every day going to be like this? I guess it's true what they say about Amsterdam!"' But of course not every day is like Queen's Day (King's Day) in Amsterdam. Even in Amsterdam, it's not the same everywhere you go. If you want the true meaning of the holiday, go to where the kids are. In my experience, it's the best selection of flea market items. And it's a wondrous celebration of creativity as the kids try to earn your loose change. They'll play drums or dance ballet. They'll offer elaborate games of skill. And they'll even give quirky high-concept performances. I once encountered a group of girls around the age of ten. They were asking 50 cents to look inside a tent labeled 'Peep show!' This seemed all kinds of wrong. But they got my 50 cents, I stuck my head in the tent, and there was a group of girls, dressed as baby chickens saying 'Peep! Peep! Peep!' In the Netherlands, even the kids are politically incorrect.

HOUSE 4

Next came my experience 'outside the ring.' If you've ever been on the highway, looked out at the charmless '70s high-rise tower blocks and wondered 'who lives there?' – that was me. There were two nice bedrooms and a third one in bad shape. There was also a home improvement center not far away. I actually took it upon myself to renovate their third bedroom room into a guest room. It was a time of my life when I was wondering where I'd settle down: Nederland or back in America. When I found myself voluntarily renovating an apartment we were temporarily subletting, that was the sign.

This time my roommate and I were subletting from a pair of students on one condition: we had to pretend we were guests. They gave us some story about receiving funding to study and to rent the apartment. But instead of studying, they were actually renting out their apartment, taking the study money and working in Ibiza. They were what I would call rich-kid *kakkers*. And they were very clear: 'Whatever happens, do NOT tell anyone we're in Ibiza. If anyone comes to the door, tell them you're houseguests. And – whatever you do – do not let anyone from the city know you're here.' So when the city required me to give a fixed address to the *Stadsregister*, I gave their address. And they subsequently got in a lot of trouble. But don't worry: I'm sure they're now very successful in Dutch banking. Or perhaps the Building Sector.

The Dutch *Stadsregister* is now the focal point of a controversial new initiative called the Participation Contract. The Dutch government would require all immigrants – including Europeans – to sign a document pledging to uphold Dutch values. I say: Why not make the Dutch sign it too? If it's good enough for me, it's good enough for Dutch students committing rent fraud.

HOUSE 5

For a week I lived on a houseboat in the Amstel, right across from *De IJsbreker*. I'd always thought of 'Ice breaker' in terms of 'conversation starter.' But since it was November when I moved in and the river was almost freezing, I soon thought of *De IJsbreker* in terms of the ship that plows a path through the ice. There were houseboats next to us, which were the more modern structures, built on floating concrete foundations. But our houseboat was a real boat, docked to the riverbank and displacing water. I'd enter through the wheelhouse and the kitchen. Then I'd climb down the stairs to the ship's hold, which was the main floor. I remember looking out the porthole windows and seeing the water less than a meter under my nose. It seemed surreal to me. For one thing, the whole city was under sea level. To park your home under river level just seemed like tempting fate. It was actually surprisingly spacious and comfortable, but I had to move out after a week.

HOUSE 6

In 1997 I came across the nastiest apartment in Amsterdam. It was in the East on a street called *Vrolikstraat*, or 'Cheerful Street.' If anyone had ever been cheerful there, it would have been a long time ago. The place was in a row of 19th-century working class houses, some of which were being gutted and fixed up. Not ours. The front door opened, and the stairs smelled like a wet cave. The

ARE WE BOTHERING YOU?!

crooked staircase led us up to a completely empty apartment – except for the balcony, which was completely full – full – of pigeon shit. Years of pigeon shit. Pigeon shit atop stacks and stacks of pigeon shit. Our jaws dropped. There was a net to keep the pigeons out, but someone had clearly ripped a hole in it. Obviously, that someone was the pierced and unwashed woman showing us the place, who explained 'pigeons need a place to live too.' Taking note of our still-dropped jaws, she casually suggested, 'You can clean it if you want.'

Somehow, my roommate convinced me to take the place with the rationale 'we just won't go on the balcony.' And 'anyway, the floors are beautiful.' And he was right. The solid oak planks were lovely. And they were gone. When we moved in they were just… gone. That was my introduction to the Dutch version of *unfurnished*. They even take the floorboards. There was just particleboard laid over the crossbeams. 'Oh yeah, didn't we tell you? We took the floors with us.' No, they didn't tell us. But we figured it out. And we got out as soon as possible.

HOUSE 7

From the east side, I moved to the northwest in the charming neighborhood called Bos en Lommer. Here we found ourselves renting from a circus duo, named Vincent & Marli. It was a nice, big place… but there was a catch. The circus wasn't doing so well, so they'd moved into the tiny storage space upstairs, to live rent-free. The deal was: we had the place to ourselves – unless they needed to use the toilet. Or unless they needed to use the kitchen. Or unless they needed to rehearse their act in the spacious living room. To be fair, they were on the road a lot, so it was a pretty good deal for us. And when they'd rehearse, it was amazing. He was a huge dude with a Hans Klok hairdo, and she was a tiny Eastern European girl with a lot of makeup. We'd wake up, hung over, on Saturday mornings, and he'd be throwing her all over the place. We loved it.

HOUSE 8

Vincent and Marli started getting paid more, so they moved back downstairs and kicked us out. That was around the time I fell in love with a Dutch woman – who owned her own apartment. I moved in almost immediately. The apartment was also in Bos en Lommer, on the third floor, above a tram stop. Our downstairs neighbors were from Aruba, from a family that seemed to keep growing. The father was a brown, pudgy man with wild hair and a penchant for loud Latin music. Music with a lot of bass. He wasn't the only one in the family with this condition. One day their family had grown into the storage space above us with a teenage boy who liked deep house – with a lot of bass. We'd just had our first child, and our bedroom was being bombarded constantly from above and from below. We'd be polite and knock on the door below. The father would always accommodate by turning the music down – not realizing that the bass was still as prominent as ever. This process repeated itself constantly.

One Saturday afternoon, we'd finally gotten our six-month-old to lie down for a nap, when the bass kicked off again from below. Our daughter woke up right away. This time we thought we'd do something different. We'd all go downstairs to knock on the door. We weren't sure what the neighbor was doing with the music so loud on a Saturday afternoon, but we soon found out. When he whipped open the door and said 'YES?' ... he was stark naked. With a condom in his hand.

But, apparently, he hadn't expected to see me AND my wife. And he certainly didn't expect a six-month-old girl. 'OK, I'll turn it down,' he said. 'NO,' my wife insisted. 'Leave it. Leave it JUST like it is, and come with me.' The naked neighbor trudged upstairs with us, and we ushered him into our bedroom, being bombarded by sound waves. It was at that moment that he got it. Months' worth of sympathy and shame flooded his eyes, as he said '*Nou – da's wel gehorig.*' Yes, it's pretty loud. He looked at us with a quizzical expression that seemed to say 'How did you survive?' We looked back at him, equally quizzically – saying 'We don't know.' And then he went to put some clothes on.

HOUSE 9

Soon after we solved the noise issue, we were invited to leave our apartment. A developer wanted to renovate the building, and he wanted to pay us to go. So we went. We'd already identified the house of our dreams, and we wanted to buy it. In fact, the owners were selling the entire building. Did we happen to know anyone who might want to buy the building with us? As it happened, the answer was yes: my father in-law. He was looking to buy a house around the same time we were. He liked the place, and he wanted to go in on it with us. Would I be willing to move in with my wife's family? It all seemed so 'Old Europe.' On the plus side, I was looking at my father in-law and thinking 'live-in babysitter.' He was looking at me and thinking 'compulsive stoop-cleaner.'

We ended up having to do some renovations to get the new place ready. That would involve us moving into my father in-law's old house on the Hemonystraat for six months. Meanwhile, he would move into the finished part of the new place to supervise the work. He'd convinced us that the normal contractors were too expensive and the cheaper Eastern European workers were just as good. I remember a van with the logo '*Bouwen met Polen*' (building with the Polish). Next to the logo was a picture of a man tearing things down. Not the best marketing campaign.

HOUSE 10

We finally moved into our new home in June, 2003. We surveyed the work, which seemed mostly good. True, the shower on the third floor turned out not to have been properly sealed and we'd later have to pay for years of hidden water damage. True, my father in-law's bathroom had been tiled with the shiny bit sticking to the wall. And when we moved in they weren't finished yet. Specifically, there were big nails sticking out of the fence where our kids would play. 'No problem!' said the Russians, who were working on that particular project.

The Russians just needed to go out for some supplies. They announced that they needed to drive over to the hardware store, and they'd be right back. They were not right back. After a few hours, they showed up, battered and traumatized. There had been a car accident. The accident had involved a tram. In his heavy Russian accent, our man explained exactly what had happened: 'The tram – it came out of nowhere!'

Despite the rails in the middle of the street – normally a pretty clear indicator of where the tram might be coming from – the Russians had been foiled! The only question on my mind was: at what point had they started drinking? Perhaps they'd started drinking after the accident to calm their nerves. Or perhaps they'd been drinking before that. Either way, the smell of vodka was wafting off of them with every failed attempt to explain.

Soon, they'd conjured up an image of the tram having willed itself off its rails in a long-contemplated act of liberating spontaneity. Needless to say, no work got done that day. But I couldn't help sympathizing with the Russians. After having dealt with magically gift-wrapped dish sets, disappearing floorboards and living room circus acts – who's to say that there are no Flying Trams in Amsterdam?

Vigilantis Security
When you want security that obeys no laws, choose Vigilantes.

CHAPTER 19

The Real Henk & Ingrid

Shapiro Turns Racist.

– Geenstijl.nl

I read it on the Internet, so it must be true: I'm racist. It's a lovely conversation-starter.

It was a long, summer day. Geert Wilders had just been voted into the top 3 parties in the Netherlands. On the day Wilders demanded to join the coalition talks, there was an attack on my house. While I was not a supporter of Wilders, I couldn't help but notice: the kid who tried to break into my house appeared to be Dutch-Moroccan.

I was in the back of the house, putting the kids to bed, but it was still light outside. We heard two loud bangs, like someone kicking our front window frames. Exactly like that, in fact. I popped my head out to spot a young man in front of my house, talking on his phone with an exaggerated casualness. He was walking across to his three friends, sitting on a bench with exquisite haircuts. As I found out later from the police, there's a standard technique on the rise. It involves a gang of kids – many Dutch-Moroccan – who kick at people's windows during the day. If the windows open a crack, they come back at night.

It was indeed a good strategy. After hearing my window being kicked and the frame cracked, I opened my door to see who was there. My first instinct was to ask the kid if he'd seen anything, but I didn't want to interrupt him on the phone. I'm from the Midwest, you know.

I have fairly good relationship with the teenage kids in my neighborhood. Some of them are Dutch-Moroccan, which I know because I've asked them. Sometimes I'll see them congregating on my stoop. I can't blame them, it's an attractive stoop. I even tease them sometimes:

'Are you *Probleem-jongeren?* Or just *Hang-jongeren?*' ['problem kids' or 'loitering kids']

They all protest 'We're just *Hang-jongeren!* ... We want a place to hang out! We don't want to cause problems.'

I tell them, 'Don't leave a mess.'

And we're all good.

My policy of engagement was inspired by Job Cohen. As Amsterdam Mayor, he advocated drinking tea together before judging each other. As a national Labor Party candidate, Cohen thus allowed tea-drinking to become a symbol of liberal weakness. What is it about tea parties that drives us to political extremes?

The kids who tried to break in to my house were ones I didn't recognize. They were the few bad apples, who were spoiling it for the bunch. Had they no idea what was going on in that day's news? Were they deliberately trying to prove Wilders right?

With that in mind, I wrote a blog piece: 'Why can't I trust my non-racist instincts?'

'Why couldn't it be NOT a Dutch-Moroccan teenager who cracked my window-frame? Why does he have to ruin it for the peaceful kids on my street? Why couldn't I see this guy in front of my house and think, "Shame on me for suspecting him?" Why do I now have to call the police and report the incident? Why do I have to add to the statistics that VVD or PVV will use to kick out immigrants who look like him? Why do I now have to help the argument that will keep out the refugees who are NOT looking for a handout, who DO want the crap jobs that the Dutch unemployed won't touch, AND who work twice as hard as everyone else? ... If I EVER see that damned kid again, I'll grab him by the neck – and make him drink tea with me.'

And that's what it takes for a blog to go viral. The website geenstijl.nl saw my blog and wrote an item about it: 'Shapiro Turns Racist After Break-in.'

It was the kind of article that starts out, 'Maybe you know Shapiro from his unfunny work on Comedy Central, his boring commentary on BNRfm, or his obnoxious commercials for ANWB.' At first I couldn't believe they could be so insulting! But I quickly realized they talk that way about everyone. So it's basically decent publicity, but couched in nastiness. Bittersweet, to be sure. But that was nothing compared to the online comments.

Geen stijl basically translates to 'No class.' You can imagine the tone of most of the comments. To be taken seriously, it's best to start out with a personal insult.

Here are some samples:

'Hey Jackass! You're racist. Islam is responsible for more violence than any religion.'

'Hey, Dumbass! If you love Morocco so much, why don't you move there?'

'Hey, F... Face! I got a tip for you: go back where you came from, and take those criminal Moroccans with you. You deserve them.'

If I had been stupid enough to respond, I would have said: 'Thank you! Thanks for pointing out who's racist. Don't forget: when accusing someone of racism, please bring out all your latent racism.'

Other comments had some intelligent points: 'Blaming Wilders is easy. ...You treat the immigrant as a noble savage. ...Or you could treat him like you would treat everybody else and expose him to law and order.'

Fair point. No rebuttal. I just thought I'd share with you the one that didn't start out using the word *ass*.

And then there was this one, which amounts to a whole separate blog piece. I have no record of who wrote it, but he was pretty specific [I left the spelling intact]:

'I just want to say that I am 100% Dutch, 19 years old. I stopped going to school to experience the life of a working class citizen. I got a job at a factory... had to redo pallets for supermarkets. I worked with two Africans, one from Kenya, the other from

South-Africa (30 years old, living here since he was 2, and doesn't talk understandable Dutch).
...Those two africans, they redid one pallet in half an hour. Me and the other whiteguy only took about 10 minutes per pallet. ... So what you say is untrue, the working class of the Nehterlands is really hard working, and we also do the crappy jobs
Now I do want you to know, I am not racist, yes I did make slave jokes to the other white guy, yes sometimes I say 'kut marokaan' without me knowing if he is truely morocan, and yes I voted VVD. And I have dated colored girls, and have colored friends. And I do not care where they come from, as long as they are honest, polite and hard-working.'

What a rebuttal! Personal narrative, very strong. But then the conclusion:

'... Racism is part of everyone, even the black people. It's fucking normal, and fucking okay.'

So you see? It doesn't matter that anyone's racist, because 'racism is fucking okay.'

The attempted break-in wasn't the only incident that occurred while Wilders was on the rise. Just a couple months after the attempted break-in, there was a fight in my daughter's classroom. Who started it? The Dutch-Moroccan kid.

It was the fall of 2010, right around the time Geert Wilders was preparing for his role in the Dutch government. My nine-year-old daughter came home and said something awful had happened at school. It was so bad that the parents were called in for a special meeting with the school director. While the politicians were debating the rules for the nation, we found ourselves having the same debate for just one boy.

The meeting started with the school director acknowledging how unusual and awkward it was. Normally, she would never invite all the parents to discuss just one boy. Especially with the boy's parents right there in the room. What she didn't acknowledge was the awkwardness of the boy's ethnicity. He was the one boy in the class with two Moroccan parents. Of course, it wasn't necessary to acknowledge it out loud, since the awkwardness was as palpable as a grip on my groin.

The politically correct director handed over to the very politically correct teacher, who seemed like she had a confession to make. She explained that the boy, Mo, had a history of anger management issues. That was no secret. Mo had been in my daughter's class since pre-school. She knew early on to keep her distance. For the record, Mo had a brother, who was a sweet kid and totally different. But in my experience as well – I'd been on school trips with the class – Mo was the most high-strung and high-maintenance in the group.

Next, the teacher explained her strategy for dealing with Mo. She hated to use terms like 'Special-needs,' but Mo often required 'special attention.' She explained how the class had learned to take a collective responsibility for him and 'care for him just as we care for each other.' In this context, I couldn't help thinking it was like a parody of Labor Party talking points.

Then the teacher explained what had really happened: she had allowed a group of boys to go to the library, including Mo. Normally, there's an adult in the library, but that day there wasn't. Despite the school motto 'Become who you are,' Mo had begun teasing one of the boys for 'having long hair, looking like a girl and being homo.' Then the fighting broke out. One student ran to get the teacher, she arrived and broke up the fight.

And what happened next was hard to explain.

The teacher gave Mo a time-out. She told him to he could come back if he calmed down. Then – she went to the Teachers Lounge for a cup of tea. As parents, we were left to wonder, 'Why on earth would she choose that moment for a coffee break?'

Moreover, was she now admitting that this was a bad decision? Or was she somehow defending her decision, because she'd had an (unjustified) faith in Mo to do the right thing? Again, it was like watching a debate with Geert Wilders and Job Cohen. Or – more accurately – Job Cohen debating himself.

What had happened next was this: with the teacher gone, Mo went back in the class and started fighting again. Again, there was no adult present. The rest of the class 'cared for each other' by telling Mo to stop fighting. That's when Mo threatened to kill everyone in the class. He picked up a chair, stood on a table, and threw the chair – which barely missed my daughter. Mo then left the class and ran out of the building, an unchecked danger to others and to himself.

How could the situation have gotten so out of hand? Did the school really think that good intentions were enough? Of course, the teacher and director apologized and explained their plans to do things differently.

But then one of the parents raised his hand: 'Is it fair to anyone that Mo should stay in this school?'

And then the real debate broke out. Some parents resisted blaming the kid. Most parents felt awkward about Mo's parents being right there. Some parents protested that love was the answer, and we just needed more of it.

And then someone brought politics into it: 'With the insidious advance of right-wing politics in Den Haag, this discussion is unconscionable. If we expel the only Moroccan in the class, we are no better than the right-wing ideologues, who are using hate to divide this country.'

I remembered feeling sensitive to that argument, but at the time it felt out of place. If anything, I wanted to know why politicians were not offering more budget for the school to provide adequate library staff, adequate adults in the building, or the remedial teaching that Mo needed.

Eventually, the debate came around to the theme of fairness. As one parent put it: 'Everyone in the class has tried to be fair to Mo, knowing that he's "easily prickled." It's gotten so bad that in gym class, if one team is beating Mo's team, they can't cheer for fear of upsetting him.'

It was unfair to subject Mo to a setting where further prickles were inevitable. And it was certainly unfair that the rest of the students should be given death threats in their classroom. As the only American in the room, I could only think of the situation in American schools, and I was glad that here they'd only been threats.

And then the school director turned it over to the parents. The school had decided that Mo would be suspended and likely moved to another school. Was there anyone who objected? Mo's parents objected. But no one else did.

Again, I was left to wonder, 'Why now?' I'd been living peacefully in my neighborhood for eight years without a break-in. Geert Wilders places third in the national election, and my house is attacked. Why now?

The Dutch-Moroccan kid in my daughter's class was trouble, but never life-threatening. Why did Mo wait all this time to freak out? Why now?

Was it just coincidence? Were they intent on proving Geert Wilders right? Or was Wilders creating some kind of self-fulfilling prophecy?

Geert Wilders became known for his quotes about 'Henk & Ingrid' – his definition of the prototypical Dutch couple. 'We're for Henk & Ingrid in this country; not for Ali & Fatima,' said Wilders. Of course, he was just generalizing. Can you imagine if there would be a real couple, who just happened to be named Henk & Ingrid? And what if they lived in, say, Almelo? And what if they'd happen to get into a fight with their neighbor, who happened to be Turkish, and he happened to end up dead?

That's what happened in 2012. A Dutch couple got into a fight with their Turkish neighbor, they bashed his head against the pavement and reportedly yelled, 'Go to hell, you dirty Turk.' Would they have felt quite so violent if their names weren't Henk & Ingrid? We'll never know.

That incident got me thinking about another episode, one of my first encounters with Dutch-Moroccan kids.

I was biking home after work, late on a Friday night. I'd had a good show, I was buzzed after a few beers, and I was making my way back to Bos en Lommer. It was a nice summer night, meaning there was no wind or rainstorm for a change. And I thought I might try calling my brother in LA. I got his voicemail, so I left a drunken message… which was abruptly cut off. Why? Read on.

There's a spot along the Jan van Galenstraat, where you never know what to expect. You can either risk your life with the trucks on the main road. Or you can risk your life on the side road with whoever's coming out of the dodgy dance club, the grow-your-own-weed shop, or the Febo. Tonight, I chose the side road, where a group of young guys was walking in the street. They were taking up the middle of the street, when the sidewalk was wide open and inviting. So perhaps, yes, there was a little extra attitude in my bell-ringing. And I should have predicted that – instead of making way – they'd block the street even more.

What happened next is best described in the voicemail my brother saved and played for me later: 'Tring-tring. TRING! TRING! "Pas op! HEY! Whaaaa!" CRASH! Thump. Tring… <Beep-beep-beep> *This call has been disconnected.*'

Here's the play-by-play. Just as the group opened up a bit to let me through, one of the guys elbowed me and knocked me off my bike. And they kept on going. When I got back up again, I was livid. And stupid. The fact that there were five of them made no difference to my righteous sense of indignation. I yelled after them, '*Aso's*!' This is short for *asociaal*, and is more accurate than insulting. I was just proud of myself that I was yelling it in Dutch. One of the gang turned and walked back to me. 'What did you say?!'

I repeated myself. And – to his surprise as well as mine – I threw myself onto him, wrestling him to the street. Mercifully, his friends were equally stunned. For some reason, they didn't start kicking the shit out of me. The reason became apparent as a police car pulled up, and the fight was over as soon as it had started. The police officers split us up and took each of us aside. I was a tall, white man in a suit. He appeared to be a teenage Dutch-Moroccan, accompanied by more teenage Dutch-Moroccans. It didn't take long for the police to choose sides. Before the police let me go, they did yell at me for behaving like an idiot.

I could have been killed. Worse, I could have killed him. Then I'd have had to change my name to Henk or Ingrid.

Of course, that was years before Geert Wilders was in power. And now that he's out of power, I've personally had less trouble with Dutch-Moroccan kids. What does that prove?

If anything, it proves that I am only a half-assed sociologist. It's also pretty clear that I am a lazy idealist, a part-time pessimist, a fence-straddling hypocrite, and sometimes a brawling drunk. But I hope I'm not really racist.

Ufuk Shoarma
When you want to defile your
shoarma yourself.

CHAPTER 20

Dutch Education: RACE TO THE MIDDLE!

The Dutch education system: VMBO, HAVO & VPRO. – Overheard at Expat Trade Fair

My two Dutch-American kids go to Dutch public schools, and I wouldn't have it any other way. Mostly because – having looked at the international schools – we couldn't afford it any other way. In terms of culture shock – it's been, shall we say, 'a learning experience.'

For a country with a reputation for liberalism and tolerance, Nederland's schools offered some odd first impressions – and some were spectacularly awkward. We quickly learned the difference between *black* schools and *white* schools. White schools are for white kids. Black schools are for, well, *other.* 'How can this be,' I thought. 'Can it really be that the Dutch practice school segregation?' Then it was explained to me by other Dutch parents. 'No, it's not segregated! There are white kids in the "black" schools. (It's just that I wouldn't want *my* white kids to join them.)' Maybe not so different from America, after all.

In Dutch primary schools, there are some wonderfully politically incorrect rituals. When there's a birthday, I've encountered a song called 'Hanky Panky Shanghai.' This is a song, to the tune of 'Happy Birthday,' in which the teachers will make slanty-eyed faces and make the children join in. Then there's the song about the boy who's so black he needs to carry a parasol in the sun. And don't get me started on Zwarte Piet.

One becomes sensitive to what the little ones are learning, especially when the teachers are making fun of your home country. My kids come home regularly with stories of their Dutch teachers making fun of Americans for overeating. (While this is of course true, I think the jokes are my job, thank you very much.) During geography lesson, my daughter hears about how Americans don't know much geography. (Tell that to Hillary Clinton.) (Or John Kerry.) Once – at my daughter's preschool – I was invited to sit in on Song Time for a singalong of 'Berend Botje.' There's a part at the end with the refrain 'America, America.' And – since this was around the time America had just invaded Iraq – the teacher sang 'America' with a big Thumbs Down gesture, stuck out her tongue, and encouraged the kids to do the same. I mentioned to the teacher later, 'You know I'm from America.' She said, 'I know.'

Don't get me wrong – I love Dutch schools. The price difference between public and private schools here is not as severe as the US. It allowed us to choose a primary school in Amsterdam, which in America would be called 'Waldorf,' and would cost thousands of dollars a year. Another positive is that there's not the disparity between rich and poor kids that I grew up with. And of course there's not the specter of school shootings that we have in America.

But for me, one of the oddest cultural distinctions of Dutch schools is the latent Calvinism that teaches children 'don't rock the boat.' Yes, the Dutch are a very tolerant people ... as long as you '*doe normaal*.' Just act normal. And it starts when they're young. My daughter started taking ballet lessons and getting good at it. But she seemed to be experiencing resentment, including from her teacher. I asked one of the other parents why this could be happening. I heard: '*Hoge bomen vangen veel wind*,' or 'the further you advance, the more resistance you get.' In essence, the lesson seems to be: *don't try*.

Next, it was at my son's school that I encountered the phrase '*Steek je hoofd niet boven het maaiveld uit (anders wordt-ie afgehakt)*.' In other words: 'Don't stick your neck out, or your head will be chopped off.' So yes, the Dutch are tolerant and free. … But if you take any chances in life, you may be executed.

This theme got really interesting when my daughter was offered a spot at the Dutch National Ballet Academy. To accept the spot, she'd have to leave her class early and switch to a different school. My American family reacted with cheers: 'That's amazing.' Also: 'So proud!' And: 'Awesome!'

My Dutch family reacted differently: 'Uh-oh … that sounds like a big change.' Also: 'That's a tough business, isn't it?' And: 'Are you sure you're not just forcing your dreams on her?' And – yes – these are all questions we'd asked ourselves as parents. But the fact was, our daughter had already spent too much time feeling underwhelmed by her old class. She demanded more challenging coursework, more stimulation, more education. So she moved.

We still bump into the parents from the old school, and they ask about my daughter. At first, I'd tell them the truth: 'It's fine, she's having a great time!' And they would frown and shake their heads. Now I tell them 'It's heavy. Lots of work. Really hard on her.' That's when they respond with a satisfied look of rueful concern. Clearly, this is a more satisfying answer for the Dutch.

And who am I to rock the boat?

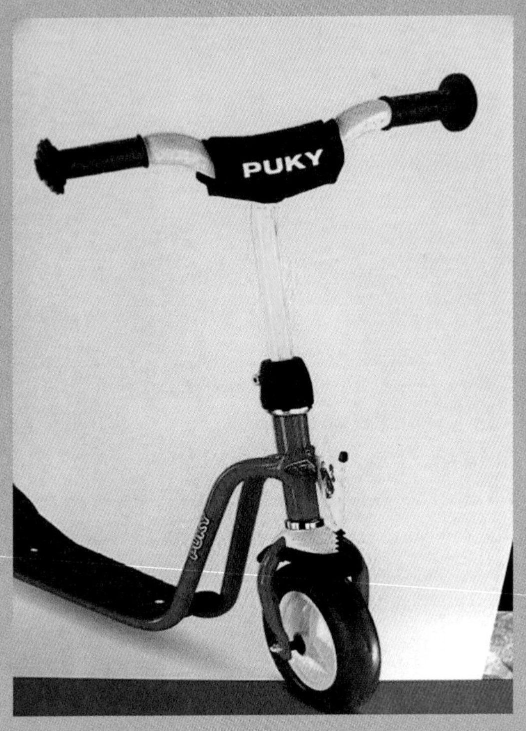

Puky

Hey kids, who wants to spin around
for 5 minutes and then puke?

CHAPTER 21

'Benefit Tourism,' Meet 'Brain Drain'

I don't think we can protect the Jews.
– Frits Bolkestein, VVD politician

I've been reading the headlines, and I know I'm supposed to be wary of 'Benefit Tourism,' aka 'Welfare Tourism.' First there were the waves of Polish immigration, next the waves of Romanians and Bulgarians. If we're not careful, we'll have untold thousands of uncultured bums moving in and mooching. There's a similar problem I've noticed with people who come here and might want to work. If the culture is inhospitable, they may want to leave. There's a difference between these two problems: one of them exists already. One of them doesn't.

Of course, I'm biased. But I can't ignore the OECD report that the costs of immigration have been greatly overstated, and the benefits of immigration outweigh the costs. A 2013 report from the Dutch statistics bureau CBS says most Europeans in the Netherlands are supporting themselves, thank you. Of the 600,000 non-Dutch Europeans who live in the Netherlands, only 6,000 live on welfare. That's 1%.

But what about this generous Dutch welfare state? Isn't it a target for asylum-seekers? For example, there were a bunch of asylum seekers in *De Vluchtkerk* in Amsterdam. I was there, speaking to an activist friend of mine. She said, 'Don't worry! Most asylum-seekers do all they can to avoid the Netherlands. Even among human traffickers, the Netherlands has a reputation for being the most inhospitable system. It's the indefinite detentions, prison brutality, and sometimes your prison burning down – with you in it.' (See: Schiphol Prison fire, 2005.) Knowing all this, I wondered why the Dutch government isn't more relaxed about immigration. She said, 'I think they have no idea.'

The Amsterdam Expat Center would seem to agree. I was talking with the Expat Center director about the expat tax incentive 'the 30% rule.' The previous government wanted to scrap the tax exemption, saying that internationals don't need such an incentive. The Expat Center director went to talk to his bosses in Den Haag to complain. Apparently, they were under the impression that most 'expats' are Shell employees on expense accounts, spending half the year in Singapore and playing golf. Really.

But elsewhere, the message is getting through. I went to a seminar at Randstad Recruiting, where even old, white men are preaching diversity. The seminar was hosted by DutchVersity (as in *Dutch Diversity*). Dutchversity was started by a young woman named Dionne Abdoelhafiezkhan (as in *Abdul, have a scan*). As it was explained to me, Dionne made a name for herself with a little experiment. To test the Dutch job market, she applied for ten different jobs with her birth name. And she applied for the same jobs with her mother's name *De Vries*. De Vries got six responses.

Abdoelhafizkhan got zero. After making her experiment public, she now has the attention of multinationals, such as Randstad.

Mr. Randstad, Ton Hopmans, is a good ol' Dutchie. He's as white and late-fifties as you can get. Hopmans: 'Looking at me, you'd think I voted for (ruling party) VVD, right?' (That's exactly what I'd thought.) 'Wrong!' And he came out swinging with a wake-up call for the Dutch government: 'The Dutch population is dying!' And it's a well-known fact: the Dutch population is getting older, having less babies, and shrinking. The Dutch call it *vergrijzing* – literally 'The Greying.' And it's a trend affecting the whole of Western Europe. According to Hopmans, by the year 2030 – probably sooner – every country in Western Europe will be 'competing for immigrants.' Not kicking them out; *inviting them in.*

Yet, if you listen to the Dutch government, *vergrijzing* isn't on the radar. Why is no one talking about this problem? Perhaps the Dutch government knows that there's only one solution to *vergrijzing*. I guess you could call it *verbruining:* the 'Browning.'

Yet, given the threat of Brain Drain, the last thing you'd want to do is scare internationals into leaving. Not long ago, VVD politician Frits Bolkestein suggested that Jews might want to leave the Netherlands because Islamic anti-Semitism is getting out of control. I'm sure the man had his reasons for going public with such a statement. But to me it seemed like the average Scooby-Doo plotline: 'I admit it! I was trying to scare everyone so they'd stay away! And I would have gotten away with it, too…'

The same day that Bolkestein made his statement, I happened to be at an event called Jewish / Moroccan Comedy night. They said the Mayor might show up. (They always say that.) But that day the Mayor did show up. PvdA Mayor Eberhard van der Laan gave a speech, blasting the VVD 'scare tactics.' He even ended with a personal plea: 'If anyone here is so afraid you're seriously thinking of emigrating, please talk to me first. Call my office. I'll take the call, 24 /7.' It wasn't a great way to end a comedy night, but the crowd liked it.

While 'Benefit Tourism' may be a real issue for some politicians, it's nice to see some people who are focused on 'Brain Drain.' Enter NUFFIC – the Dutch organization for international students in the Netherlands. Recently, they organized an entire trade fair with the explicit goal of keeping these students in the country. I spoke at the event and did a quick poll. 'How many of you are hoping to stay after you graduate?' Most of the 500 people had their hands up. So at least their strategy seems to be working.

I spoke to one woman from Manhattan. She was a dyed-in-the-wool New Yorker. She'd lived there all her life, thought of Manhattan as the pinnacle of civilization, and never thought of leaving. But then she wanted to get her Master's Degree. Columbia University wanted $50,000. University of Amsterdam offered a similar program for much less.

Come to think of it, there were a lot of Europeans in the audience at NUFFIC. I spoke to a Polish woman studying psychology. A Greek woman was studying Business Management. And yes, there was a Romanian woman. She was doing research at an

NGO. She was with some other Romanians. I asked if they were worried about next year, when the floodgates of Romanians and Bulgarians are due to open wide. The Romanians said 'YES! Bulgarians are stupid!' I also spoke to some Bulgarians, who said 'UGH! Romanians think they know everything!' So – given the classic rivalry between the Netherlands and Belgium – they should fit right in.

Pull & Bear
'Is this where you do the bikini waxing?'

CHAPTER 22

Dutch Service – an Oxymoron?

The Dutch are historically a non-hierarchical society. Since they overthrew the Spanish in the 1500s, they make it a point not to take orders from anyone.

– Ton Heibergs, Royal Tropical Institute

The term 'Dutch service' can be an oxymoron. In keeping with their non-hierarchical tradition, the rationale of Dutch service is often: 'Don't tell me what to do.'

In Dutch restaurants, I've had the following conversations:
Me: 'Excuse me, is it possible to turn up the heat a bit?'
Waiter: 'Why?'
Me: 'I'm cold.'
Waiter: 'I don't think so.'

Me: 'Excuse me, could I send this item back to the kitchen?'
Waiter: 'Why?'
Me: 'I think it's not cooked properly.'
Waiter: 'Yes it is.'

Me: 'Check, please?'
Waiter: (cleaning behind the bar, avoiding eye contact)
Me: 'Hello, could we have the bill, please?'
Waiter: (going for smoke break, avoiding eye contact)
Me: 'Please, can we pay?'
Waiter: (eventually delivers the check)
Me: 'Finally... we could have walked out about three times by now.'
Waiter: (angrily) 'Well, why didn't you, then?!'

In the Netherlands, 'The Client is King.' But not the boss. Just like the King.

I'd always thought that America was a land of rugged 'do-it-yourself' types, and Europe was more about overbearing wait staff. But in fact it's America where you're bombarded with 'Can I help you?' And in the Netherlands, when you want to order, you're on your own.

On a sunny day in Amsterdam, the work just stops as everyone makes their way to a café terrace. Everyone is drinking and soaking up the sun. And there's probably someone smoking right next to you. And you can't actually get a drink. Because the one next to you with the cigarette is your waiter. Shouldn't they be serving drinks? 'Nah, the sun is out.'

Where do the Dutch learn their customer service skills? There's actually quite a lot of training for the hospitality industry. For example, there's the Hotel School in Amsterdam West. It's the one where the smoking area is located right outside the front entrance. So for anyone passing by, it appears that an integral part of service training is SMOKE BREAK.

The very term 'Dutch hospitality' can get you into trouble. Even when people invite you over, it's by appointment only. I've met Dutch people who say, 'You simply must come visit!' But make sure you don't drop in unannounced. When I first got here, I took up my neighbor's offer to drop by sometime, but they were about to have dinner. 'No problem,' he said. 'While we're eating our dinner, you can sit in the other room and read a magazine. Smells good, huh?'

The concept of tipping is quite different in America and the Netherlands too. One of our favorite places in the Netherlands is Café Restaurant Amsterdam. We'll frequently go there after returning from the States. Our servers are attentive and work as a team. When we ate there last, I was paying the bill, and my American tipping instincts took over:

'15% of 68 euros is upwards of 10. So I'll give 80 euros to be safe.'

My Dutch wife protested, 'No! They'll think you're trying to be some kind of rich asshole. Just round up!'

'Fine, I said. 'I'll give 70.'

'Perfect.'

'Are you sure? Two euros tip on a bill of 68?'

And – sure enough – when I gave the two euros, they looked genuinely surprised and said 'Thank you!'

Whereas – in America – they'd try to claw my eyes out.

In America, the sales stereotype is 'ABC: Always Be Closing.' In Nederland, it's just a bit different.

My wife got a gift coupon to shop at a *parfumerie*. It was full of 'handmade scents' and little cards for spraying and testing the

perfumes. After a few minutes, the shopkeeper came up and said, 'Can't you spray that outside? I have to work here all day, and it gives me a headache!' It was suggested that perhaps the woman might want to find another line of work. As it turned out, she didn't just work in the shop. She was the owner.

A friend of mine was trying on boots in Den Haag. She finally found the pair she was looking for, but the man behind the counter announced, 'We're almost closed.' My friend asked if she could just check if they had the right size? The shopkeeper returned with the right sized boots, and my friend went to try them on. She took off her shoes and tried on the left boot, when the shopkeeper turned off the lights.

'We're closing,' he said.

'Uh-oh,' my friend said. 'I guess I'll quickly try on the other boot…'

'I said we're closed,' said the man.

My friend protested, 'Can I just pay for them right now?'

'Sorry. The cash register is shut down.'

'But I want to buy the boots.'

'Then you should have come earlier,' he said. And he kicked her out of the shop. Sometimes making a sale is not as important as shaming the customer.

My father was staying at a bed & breakfast in the Jordaan. The owner was apparently a former psychotherapist. This is what my father found out when staying there. My dad reported many interesting chats in the mornings. The owner would put out a traditional Dutch breakfast and just observe my father as he ate. At the end of his stay, the owner asked my father if he would like to come stay again at the B&B. My father said, 'Well, sure, I think I might come back and stay here again.' The owner looked him straight in the eye and said 'No you won't.' And he was right.

I was entering a café and opened the door for a Dutch woman. She was so taken aback by my gesture that she stopped in her tracks and said, 'I'm not going to fuck you.'

But there are signs of improvement. A glass of tap water will be provided free of charge at the café these days. Not long ago, tap water was inexplicably off-limits. A new generation of Dutch retail staff seem to care a bit more about their work. And I've personally given 'Customer Friendliness' trainings to Schiphol Duty Free staff. (But I can't vouch for any results there.)

It's also true that American service is not always so admirable. I was expecting more American-style service when I went to New York recently. But the stereotypes don't always hold true. There are definitely a couple of places in Manhattan where 'a New York minute' translates into 'quarter of an hour.' The bike rental shop guys were quite friendly, but they were in a different time zone. And we even found a Belgian beer place, serving *frites* with mayonnaise… beer, *frites* AND bad service? Why did I need to leave Europe?

And of course Dutch people point out the negative stereotypes about American service. Americans say, 'Have a nice day' and 'How are you doing?' And they don't really care.

But there's one thing worse. When they actually DO care.

I was back in the US for a mini family reunion. It was a theme restaurant outside Chicago with my dad and my brothers, whom I hadn't seen in two years. We got a back room all to ourselves, which was great. The only problem was a little attention-starved freak called our waitress.

'Hi! My name is Ariel, and I'll be your server today! If there's anything you need at any point, feel free to let me know. Would you like to hear our specials today?'
'No,' we said.
'Okay, well, here they are anyway… ' And she went on to tell us the whole menu.

We ordered as quickly as possible, so I could catch up with my brothers. One of them is a screenwriter in LA. I asked, 'Is it true your script is getting financed? And you're going to direct?' I want to hear more!

And here was Ariel again: 'How's everything with your meals?'…

(…Granted, this is a question you never get to hear in a Dutch restaurant. Until after the meal. The term '*Heeft het gesmaakt?*' means 'Did it taste good?', but it really means: 'I hope you're done, because I'm taking your plate.' For fun, you can tell them the food was not perfect and maybe even give them a message for the kitchen, such as 'too much salt.' And the Dutch waiters will stand there staring at you, until you get your line right: 'You're supposed to say: "It was *lekker*."')

Again, just as I was getting caught up with my brother, here was Ariel again: 'Did you guys want to order any extra fries or side dishes at this time?'

'No, thank you.' Anyway, my brother was already doing a bit of casting for the movie, and he was getting some interest from some big names.

Ariel: 'Do you guys want any refills?'

The drinks were enormous already. I felt like I was getting diabetes just looking at the cola.

'No thank you.' My brother told me that there was an Oscar winner who wanted to star in his movie. Who was it!?

Ariel again: 'I went ahead and brought you guys some more drinks just in case. Let me just make some room for you…'

And I was the one who decided to use my Dutch bluntness. I said, 'You know what? We don't want drinks right now. We just want the chance to finish our conversation. I don't know if you can tell, but we're having a little family reunion.'

Ariel chimed in, 'OH! Family reunion! That's nice. My family is all from right around here, so we see each other constantly. I guess you could say we have a family reunion all the time. My brother says he wants to go away to school...'

I couldn't believe it. Why on earth did she think I wanted to skip hearing about my own family so I could hear about hers?

I said, 'Sorry – maybe I've been unclear. I don't get to see these guys very often. I live in Amsterdam.'

Wrong move. Ariel continued, 'OH! Amsterdam! I'd love to go to Amsterdam. I keep saying I have to get over there someday to see Amsterdam, because that's my name: ARIEL! I just want to see that statue of the Little Mermaid.'

I had to admit: I was dying to get back to Dutch service. I was dying to ask for a drink and have the waiter tell me to fuck off.

*

There's something about Dutch service that I've found to be integral to the Dutch experience. I remember the day I had this realization. It was when we had to get a new washing machine.

Here's the story. Our old washing machine broke down. So we went to the *witgoed* store, or the 'White, good store.' If the appliances are white and good, they've got 'em. We shopped around for different brands, and we ended up doing what every good Dutch couple does: we bought a German machine. It was the heaviest.

We told them at the store: 'Installing it may be tricky. It's going to have to go past the bathtub, over a toilet, into a little nook.'

'No problem!' was the answer. 'They will even take the old one away. That is the job of our service team.'

SERVICE TEAM. When I hear this term in the Netherlands, it sets off warning bells and red flags. Any time you hear the word *service* and *team* in Dutch, there's trouble.

We were told it should be possible. It sounded good enough. So the service team showed up. And realized our washing machine is not easy to get to. It lives in the back corner of our bathroom. We actually have a bathtub and a toilet in the same room, which is not common. So when the service team surveyed the scene, we heard that classic Dutch phrase 'Mmmm. That is not possible.' This means 'It is possible, I just don't feel like it.'

My first instinct was to play the role of the self-righteous American: 'They said at store it should be possible! Now what about customer satisfaction? I mean, we are paying you!'

But then it struck me: 'Wait a minute – no. Maybe the Dutch communicate in a different way.' I told my wife, 'Stand back, honey. I'm going to try to communicate with them.'

She said, 'Please don't try to do it in Dutch.'

But I slumped myself down next to the delivery guys and said, 'Wow, this sucks for you. Big heavy washing machine. You guys have to lift it up and over. You have to lift heavy stuff all day. Don't you? Yeah. Must be tough. You know, they said at the store that it would be possible. But I see now that it is not possible. So I guess, okay, you can go. Yeah. I guess I'll just have to do it myself. But I don't know, I might hurt my back. So I could call a neighbor or something. But what if he gets hurt, then I need insurance, which I don't have. So take it back to the truck. I guess you'll just have to return it...'

And they looked at each other, as if to say: 'Wow. That was really good complaining.'

And then they said, 'Well, okay, we'll give it a try...'

And sure enough: Bam! It was done.

That's how to really communicate with the Dutch. And they don't teach you that at the *Inburgeringscursus*.

Shabby
Only the shabbiest fashion.

CHAPTER 23

Ranking the Standards

Metric System Thriving in America's Inner Cities… from kilos of cocaine to cc's of heroin to the Glock 9mm, inner-city youths possess a firmer grasp of the metric system than their peers in suburban and rural areas.
– The Onion.com

Coming to the Netherlands from the US, I had trouble adapting to certain Dutch standards.

But taking a fresh look at the US, there are plenty of American standards that are clearly inferior. Maybe it's time to set the record straight.

Why not start with the Metric system? It's so obviously superior that even the Americans are wishing they could convert to the global standard. But then we'd have to change the name of the 'Quarter Pounder,' and that would never do.
Nederland jumps out to a quick lead.
USA 0, NED 1

But then there's the Dutch standard of counting. The Dutch still say their numbers with the 1's then the 10's. Hence, 24 is 'four-and-twenty,' which I can never say without thinking of medieval blackbirds. When Dutch people try to give you their phone numbers, it quickly gets ridiculous:

'06...'

I write down *06*.

'4 and fifty.'

I write down 45. ERASE! I go back and write it properly: *54*.

'6 and thirty.'

I write down *63*. ERASE! Sorry: *36*.

'7'

That's easy: *7*.

'3...'

I write down 3.

'... times zero.'

ERASE!

Hopeless. Point America.

USA 1, NED 1

There's the American standard of giving the date: Month/Day/Year. That's like saying Winter/Summer/Spring.

Point Nederland.

USA 1, NED 2

Quotation marks. I don't really care if you use the standard 'single' or "double." But do use them. Too many Dutch children's books have little or random quotation marks. When I'm reading to my kids, I just sound stupid.

'The farmer has chickens. Said Janneke. I like chickens. Said Jip.'

My kids protest that I'm not doing the voices right.

'No I'm not, kids, because there are no quotation marks. Good luck learning to read.'

Point America.

USA 2, NED 2

In buildings, why not start counting floors at good old number 1? There should be no such thing as 'Floor 0.' And by the way, they're *floors*. The Dutch call them *verdiepingen,* which refers to 'going deep,' while actually they're going higher. Going lower and higher at the same time? No wonder MC Escher was Dutch.

Point America.

USA 3, NED 2

Terminology. When the Dutch want a cola, they order a 'cola.' Try that in the US:

'I'd like a cola.'

'A *cola*? You mean like Coca-Cola?'

'Yes.'

'We don't have Coca-Cola.'

'What do you have?'

'Pepsi.'

'Which is a ... ?'

'Cola.'

'Which is why I ordered a *cola*.'

Point Nederland.

USA 3, NED 3

When the Dutch want a taxi, they order a 'taxi.' In the US, you get a taxi, OR you 'get a cab.' It's not just that this term is outdated. It's that the term refers to the *front seat* of a vehicle – where passengers are not supposed to sit. In most countries I've visited, if you try getting into the front seat, you're announcing that you're probably trying to rob the driver. Ironically, the Netherlands is one of the few countries where it IS okay to sit in the front. And they still don't say '*cab*.'

Point Nederland: Nederland in the lead!

USA 3, NED 4

When Dutch people aim a cameraphone at you, they don't '*take* a picture,' they '*make* a picture.' The Dutch way makes more sense. When Americans say 'I want to *take* a picture,' I always think *Airplane*, when the reporter says 'Let's take some pictures,' and they steal the photos from the walls.

Point Nederland.

USA 3, NED 5

Conversely, Dutch people don't know how to make a decision. That's because Dutch people don't *make* a decision; they *take* a decision (as do the Brits). Apparently, if you can't *make* up your mind, you need to *take* a decision – most likely from someone else. It's an especially tricky subject with politics. Ask the Dutch (or the Brits) to make a decision about the economy, and they'll take their decision from, say, Germany.

Point US.

USA 4, NED 5

The Dutch still haven't come up with a decent term for 'significant other.' I've met too many Dutch men my age, who still don't know how to refer to the female partner they've been living with for 10 years.

'This is my… girlfriend.'

'How long have you been dating?'

'We're not dating; we live together. She's like my wife.'
'How long have you been married?'
'We're not married... she's my partner.'
'So you're in business?'
'We're not in business. She's my... baby mama?'

Dutch people, you invented the term *samenwonen*. You really should figure out what to call the person you're spending your life with. Why not *samenwoman*?

Point America.

USA 5, NED 5.

Farewells. The Dutch say '*Doei*!' The Yanks say 'Bye-bye.' Both are equally silly, really. The Yanks say 'See you,' whereas the Dutch say '*tot ziens*,' or '*tot kijk*,' or '*tot zo*,' or '*tot later*,' or any number of options – which only increase the likelihood of me getting it wrong. I normally say, 'tot (mumble mumble),' so Dutch people can fill in the right one themselves. Then there's the Dutch formal farewell, '*De groeten*.' This translates to 'the greetings,' which is just backwards.

Point America.

America back in the lead.

USA 6, NED 5

Telling time. In Britain 'half-ten' is 10:30. In Nederland 'half-ten' is 9:30. The Dutch are living in the future. The Americans say 'half PAST ten,' which is on the side of the Brits. The Dutch think in terms of 'halfway to ten,' which is more forward-thinking. Then again, when I'm rushing for a train, the Dutch will hit me with bizarre phrases like '*tien over half negen*,' which means 'ten, minus 30, plus ten.' By the time I've figured that out, the train doors have closed in my face.

No points.
USA 6, NED 5

Americans have 'gas stations,' where you can get gasoline. But nowadays you can also get natural gas. And anything you eat from there will give you gas. The term 'gas station' is terribly unspecific. The Dutch have 'tank stations,' which is only confusing if you're driving a tank.
Point Nederland.
USA 6, NED 6.

Dutch people have 'mobile numbers' for their mobile phones. Americans have 'cell numbers' for their 'cellular' phones. I know 'cellular' refers to the service infrastructure, but if the abbreviation is 'cell,' it's intolerable. When I give my American friends my 'mobile number,' they laugh at me, like I'm the idiot. But *mobile number* only means one thing: mobile phone number. *Cell number* only means one thing: you are in prison. It could be worse: German mobile phones are called 'Handys,' which means something very different in American prisons.
Point Nederland.
USA 6, NED 7

I'm sure there are more examples, but as of now it's the Netherlands with more common-sense standards than the Yanks. If you're like me, you'll try to convert the Americans to say 'taxi' and 'cola' and 'mobile number.' Of course, it can be confusing when you get caught in between cultures. If this happens, remember to just relax and go your gang.

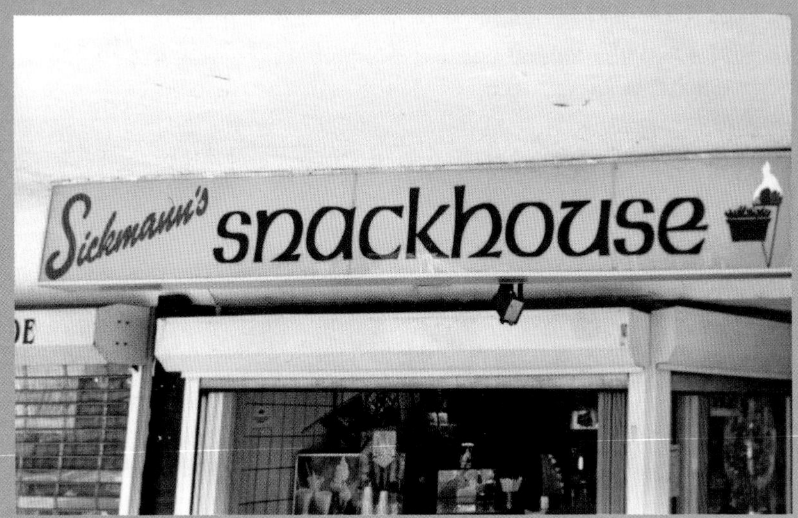

Sickmanns Snackhouse
'Achoo! Here's your order.'

CHAPTER 24

Dutch Identity: A New Ombudsman

Willem-Alexander looks good as a Queen.
– Overheard on Dam Square

As of this writing, the Dutch identity crisis is still in plain sight. According to the polls, the Dutch don't trust their leadership to steer the country out of the crisis. They no longer feel confident of their place in the European Union. And they're not as good at football (soccer) as they'd like.

There's one bright note that brings a lot of Dutch together: the Dutch Royal Family. At the abdication of Queen Beatrix, her approval was overwhelming. The investiture of King Willem-Alexander was a flawless event. A rare, international display of Dutch pride. Even the protestors gave grudging approval. The loudest anti-monarchists these days are in the Socialist Party. (Yes, Dutch Republicans are Socialist.) Instead of boycotting the Investiture or refusing to pledge their allegiance to the King, the Socialists decided not to dress up or even to wear ties. The result – where I was watching – was less 'Wow, what a statement,' but more 'Ugh, who let *them* in?'

Is this indeed what the anti-monarchist Willem van Oranje would have wanted for his country?

Sometimes I think back to that seminar on 'Dutch Identity: Who Are We?' If I could go back to that panel, there are a few things I'd like to say.

I took the assimilation course, and it was great! It might not hurt for everyone to take it, Dutch people too. Call it a universal 'Participation Contract' if you like: 'You are about to Participate in the grand experiment known as Dutch Society. Rembrandt, Leeuwenhoek, Tasman. They're all Dutch. But also Spinoza, Descartes, even Willem of Orange *van Duitsen bloed*. They're all immigrants. You've got some pretty big shoes to fill. Do your best! Sign here.'

It's all there in black & white & orange: the Netherlands is the first republic in the world. You had the world's first multinational company, the first stock exchange, the first multi-ethnic colony in the New World and the inspiration for the American Dream.

The Dutch have a lot of unique selling points in the world. Indeed – from dikes breaking to oil spilling to global warming – Dutch people have answers to a lot of the world's problems. The problem is the rest of the world doesn't know about it. The rest of the world should give the Dutch more credit. But they can't – not as long the Dutch refuse to take any credit.

Nederland, take some credit! I get it, you're Dutch: being proud is not in your DNA. But you can learn.

Stop saying 'Full is full.' If the land gets too full, you'll just make more. You're Nederland!

Stop saying 'Our economy is in trouble…' You still have some of the lowest unemployment in Europe. You're Nederland!

Stop saying you're afraid Islam is taking over your culture. You're Nederland! Half the Muslims in the world started out half-Dutch already.

Maybe the Dutch anthem really should be: 'Wilhelmus van Nassouwe; I come from German blood. And French. And Spanish. And Turkish and Moroccan and Surinamese and Indonesian and American and the more the better.'

And as proof of the benefits of cultural diversity, there's me. I'm Dutch enough to be proud of the Dutch, and American enough to not care how loud I am about it.

How to Be Orange

– The Assimilation Exam

The following questions are taken from the 'Nationale Inburgering Test' at NTR.nl. These are the closest I could find to the questions I had in my course.

To pass the test you need 5.5 out of 10. It sounds easy, but there's one group of people who traditionally have a hard time: the Dutch.

The online exam even gives you some examples of how some famous Dutch people have scored.

Jacques d'Ancona (TV journalist): 4.7
Howard Komproe (comedian): 4.6
Victoria Koblenko (soap actress): 4.0
Note: none of them achieved 5.5.
Now is your chance to prove you're more Dutch than famous Dutch people!

One year, the Dutch Assimilation Test appeared on TV. The winners were Chinese food delivery guys.

Many of the questions were not covered in my class. Nor were they covered in standard Dutch education, apparently. Nor are they particularly relevant.

But is that a bad thing? In any given classroom full of people taking this exam, there's a real sense of solidarity as everyone looks around and shrugs 'I have no idea.'

Of course, there's always been controversy around the exam. Recently, a researcher from Radboud University found that the entire process is counter-productive, in part because the exam questions are so subjective.

Yes, they're subjective: that's what makes them so perfect! A simple analysis of each question reveals more about the Dutch mentality than the exam ever intended.

*

SAMPLE QUESTION

Wat of wie herdenken wij op 4 mei?
A – Alle oorlogsslachtoffers
B – Het begin van de Tweede Wereldoorlog
C – Het einde van de Tweede Wereldoorlog.

TRANSLATION
[via Google / Shapiro]
What or who is commemorated on the 4th of May?
A – All war victims
B – The beginning of World War II
C – The end of World War II.

ANSWER = A

Most Dutch people know the 4th of May is not about the end of the war: that's the 5th of May. But many Dutch people are unclear on who exactly is being commemorated. Sometimes it's all war victims, including the Germans. Sometimes it's for everyone but the Germans. It keeps changing. One thing that doesn't change: at 8 PM, shut up.

Perhaps the more practical question would be:
HOW do the Dutch commemorate war victims on the 4th of May?
Answer: with two minutes of silence at 8 PM.

A friend of mine arrived in the Netherlands in the month April and – by the time 4 May rolled around – he was happy he could navigate the Laundromat. There he was, putting coins into the dryer and successfully turning it on. But at 8 PM, an older woman came up. She opened the door and turned the dryer off.

My friend made it clear he was using the dryer, deposited more coins and turned the dryer back on. Again, the woman opened the door and turned the dryer off. My friend was now getting angry, since again he'd lost his money. He yelled at the woman in his best Dutch, but she simply gestured for him to be quiet.

Enraged, he put more coins into the dryer, and he found himself grappling with this old woman, as she tried to open the door. She kept pointing at the clock and saying 'Shhh! Shhh!' And then – suddenly – she gave up. My friend felt victorious.

Only later did he realize he was aggressively keeping this woman from observing her annual two minutes of silence. The ironic part is my friend was the one who was Jewish.

ESSENTIAL KNOWLEDGE

It can be difficult to figure out the Dutch.
Even the Dutch can't figure out the Dutch.
You can see how each of these questions is essential knowledge.

Hoe is nootmuskaat eigenlijk in Nederland gekomen?
A – Via onze kolonie de Nederlandse Antillen
B – Via onze kolonie Nederlands-Indië
C – Via onze kolonie Suriname.

How did nutmeg first arrive in the Netherlands?
A – From OUR COLONY in the Antilles
B – From OUR COLONY Indonesia
C – From OUR COLONY Suriname.

ANSWER = B

True answer – Who cares? Are you really going to kick someone out of the country for not knowing where nutmeg comes from?

Waar is de bloemenbollensector het grootst?
A – In de provincie Flevoland
B – In de provincie Noord-Holland
C – In de provincie Zuid-Holland.

Where is the tulip bulb industry the biggest?
A – In the province of Flevoland
B – In the province of Noord-Holland
C – In the province of Zuid-Hollland.

ANSWER = B

Hopefully, if you're taking this test you're no longer picking tulip bulbs.

Hoe lang doet u er ongeveer over om met de trein, zonder vertragingen, van Amsterdam naar Enschede te reizen?

A – 1 uur

B – 2 uur

C – 3 uur.

Approximately how long does it take to travel by train – without delays – from Amsterdam to Enschede?

A – 1 hour

B – 2 hours

C – 3 hours.

ANSWER = B

For anyone getting this question wrong, you can follow up with a rebuttal:

Approximately how long does it take to travel by High-Speed FYRA train – without delays – from Amsterdam to Brussels?

A – Under 10 years

B – Over 10 years

C – We may never know.

EVERY QUESTION TELLS A STORY

It's not about answering the questions.
The real lesson is the logic behind the questions.

Een collega van u gaat trouwen. Ze geeft een klein feestje. U bent niet uitgenodigd, maar u wilt iets doen. Wat doet u?
A – U geeft een cadeau, bijvoorbeeld iets voor de keuken
B – U stuurt een envelop met geld
C – U stuurt haar een kaartje.

Your colleague from work is getting married. You are not invited to the wedding, but you want to do something nice. What do you do?
A – You give a gift, for example something for the kitchen
B – You give an envelope with money
C – You send a card.

ANSWER = C

I've asked this question to hundreds of Dutch people. When I ask why, the answer is invariably, 'Because it's cheap.'

U zit met een collega op een terras en u ziet, een tafeltje verderop, twee mannen die elkaar strelen en zoenen. U stoort zich hieraan. Wat doet u?

A – U blijft zitten en doet alsof u het niet erg vindt

B – U zegt tegen de mannen dat ze ergens anders moet gaan zitten

C – U zegt nogal luidruchtig tegen uw collega wat u vindt van homoseksualiteit.

You are sitting with a colleague at a terrace. At the table next to you there are two men kissing and caressing each other. You are bothered by this. What do you do?

A – You remain seated and act as if you are not offended

B – You tell the men that they should go sit somewhere else

C – You say loudly to your colleague what you think about homosexuality.

ANSWER = A

My favorite part of this question is the assumption: 'You are bothered by this.' Personally, I'm not bothered. But for the sake of the question, I have to be. And – after getting into the role of an offended person – perhaps C would be the most honest answer. But no – to answer the question correctly, you have to pretend to be someone who IS offended, pretending NOT to be offended.

Incidentally, most Dutch people I've met WOULD say something. It's a terrace. And they're not just kissing, they're 'kissing and caressing.' I would not be surprised to hear someone say 'Get a room, Mary!' Or at the least they'd say, '*Doe normaal!*'

This question could have been written by George Orwell. The real lesson here is 'Don't commit a Thought Crime.'

But then again, homophobia in the Netherlands is a problem. I once saw interview on AT5. Two Dutch Moroccan kids were asked what they thought of the Gay Pride Parade. One of them said: 'Somebody should tell them to go back where they came from!' Technically, that would be 'The Closet.'

There should be a better way of making such a statement sound ridiculous. Perhaps – instead of the test question – they should just play this kid's video clip.

U ruikt gaslucht in uw huurwoning. Wat moet u dan doen?
A – Alle ramen en deuren open doen en het energiebedrijf bellen
B – Alle ramen en deuren sluiten en een erkende installateur bellen
C – De hoofdkraan sluiten en de afdeling huisvesting van de gemeente bellen.

You smell gas in your rental apartment. What should you do?
A – Open all the windows and doors and call the utility company
B – Close all the windows and doors and call an accredited installation company
C – Close the gas valve and call the local housing department.

ANSWER = A

There are some very useful tips here, but they're not in the same answer.

If you open all the windows. You're rather safe.
If you also shut off the gas valve, you are very safe.
But – according to the exam – you're not Dutch.

U maakt uw frituurpan schoon en wilt het vloeibare vet weg-gooien. Waar moet u dit laten?
A – Door de WC spoelen
B – Bij je gewone afval stoppen
C – Bij het chemische afval doen.

You are cleaning out your deep fryer and you want to dispose of the frying oil. You always use liquid frying oil. What should you do with it?
A – Flush it down the toilet
B – Put it out with the rest of the garbage
C – Deliver it to the chemical disposal.

ANSWER = B

I admit… I got this one wrong. Perhaps it's because we've NEVER HAD A DEEP FRYER.

I admit… I'm not very Dutch.

But – again – the question assumes: 'You always use frying oil.' This is either because I'm Dutch, or because I'm non-western and uneducated. Either way, as someone who's nutritionally and environmentally responsible, I feel left out.

And the most unfortunate part is that the best answer isn't even on there: turn your used frying oil into bio diesel for KLM.

Bij de buren, drie huizen verderop, staat opeens een houten ooievaar in de tuin. Zij hebben daar dus een kindje gekregen. Het zijn aardige mensen en ze groeten altijd. Wat kunt u het beste, als eerste reactie, doen?

A – U doet meteen een felicitatiekaart in de brievenbus

B – U gaat direct bij de buren langs om het kindje te bewonderen

C – U wacht een paar dagen en gaat dan op bezoek.

The neighbors on your street have placed a wooden stork in their garden. They've just had a baby. You are friendly with the neighbors and they always greet you. What should you do first?

A – Put a greeting card in their postbox

B – Visit your neighbors to see the baby

C – Wait a few days and then visit the baby.

ANSWER = A

In other words: you never drop in on your neighbors. You can look through their front windows and clearly see everything they're doing. But you're not allowed to interact with them! Voyeurism only.

Even if your neighbors are very friendly, and even if they say 'You must come over sometime…' you must wait for them to pull out an agenda and say, 'Next July on Thursday the 17th. How is that for you?'

Uw vierde kindje is helemaal gezond ter wereld gekomen. U ontvangt een oproepkaart van het consultatiebureau. Wat doet u?

A – U gaat met uw kindje naar het consultatiebureau

B – U gaat niet omdat die afspraak niet verplicht is

C – U gaat niet omdat u nu wel weet hoe alles moet.

You've just had your 4th child, a healthy baby. You receive an invitation to the pediatric clinic. What should you do?

A – You go with your child to the pediatric clinic

B – You don't go because it's not required

C – You don't go because you know by now how to care for your children.

ANSWER = A

My favorite part of this question: 'You have four children.' Why is it necessary to assume I have four children? Is it part of Dutch culture to have lots of babies? Or are we assuming that I'm probably uneducated and I have nothing better to do than popping out progeny like there's no tomorrow?

On a related note, there was a question on the test taken by the Dutch author Rodaan Al Galidi: 'How long after a miscarriage does a woman resume menstruation?'

What's that got to do with cultural assimilation? Somewhere there must be an obstetrician's exam asking, 'Who painted *The Nightwatch*?'

The Dutch Ministry of *Sociale Zaken* was careful to announce that they did not develop this question. Rather, it was developed by an independent agency called ICE. *ICE* is also agency that provides high-speed rail service to Germany, proving again that immigration and German trains are a bad combination.

Je loopt op straat met je vriendin, die lastig wordt gevallen door een vreemde kerel. Wat doe je dan?

A – *Je laat het aan haar over*

B – *Je doet allebei of die man niet bestaat*

C – *Hij krijgt een klap – en zij ook!*

You are walking down the street and your girlfriend receives unwelcome attention from another man, what do you do?

A – Let her solve it herself

B – Both ignore it

C – He gets a smack – and she does too!

ANSWER = B

But thank you for assuming that I might want to hit my girlfriend.

And of course the most Dutch answer would be: if you're walking down the street and your girlfriend receives unwelcome attention from another man, charge him money.

RIGHT ANSWER vs TRUE ANSWER

It is important to know how the Dutch see themselves.
It is also important to know the truth.

Waarom zijn wij in Nederland begonnen met het aansteken van vuurwerk bij het begin van een nieuw jaar?
A – Om de kwade geesten te verjagen
B – Om Oud en Nieuw extra feestelijk te maken
C – Omdat de Chinezen dat deden. Wij hebben dat overgenomen.

How did the Dutch start the tradition of lighting fireworks on New Year's?
A – To chase evil spirits away
B – To make New Year's Eve extra festive
C – Because the Chinese did it. We took it over.

ANSWER = A

Historically, the Dutch chased away evil spirits by gathering together to make loud noises.
Again, you can see why this is essential knowledge.

TRUE ANSWER = B

For my job, I've asked this question to hundreds of Dutch people. Most of them answer B, probably because it has the most relevance to everyone's lives. But that's not what this test is about.

Whatever the historical background, the fact is that New Year's Eve in the Netherlands is an enormous party. I love bringing friends and family over for New Year's. Coming from America, we hear 'fireworks,' and we think of the 4th of July. Independence Day fireworks are coordinated by the local governments. The displays start with fireworks going off one by one, then they get a little faster, and they end with a bunch of fireworks going off all in a row.

But in the Netherlands, after the countdown '5-4-3-2-1...' it's Shock and Awe. 360 degrees of bombs bursting in air. Everyone in every street is lighting their own private stash of fireworks. We even tried it one year. As a word of caution: when you want to launch a rocket, don't do what I did.

I'd watched my neighbors using champagne bottles to launch their rockets, and I did the same – but I didn't think to fill mine with water. We lit the fuse, stood well back, and watched as the wind tipped the bottle over, just as the rocket fired. The rocket took off at about face-level and exploded in the street a block away. We looked to see if anyone was hurt, but all we saw was a single bicyclist coming towards us with a very large frown. The way I remember it is slightly cartoonish. I could swear his bike was still smoking.

I find it amazing that there's a small economic boom every year, in the form of fireworks. Everyone ends up lighting a small fortune in privately purchased fireworks.

And at the end of every year, even if the economy has slipped into recession, the Dutch have a habit of breaking new records in fireworks spending, time after time. And what better way to celebrate a crisis? Take your investments and literally watch them go up in smoke.

***Als Nederlanders landgenoten tegenkomen in het buitenland, wat doen ze?**

A – Ze respecteren elkaars privacy

B – Ze denken 'Wat leuk' en nodigen hen uit voor een lopend buffet

C – De vraag is niet van toepassing, Nederlanders gaan graag op reis met andere Nederlanders.

If Dutch people come across other Dutch people in a foreign country, what do they do?

A – They respect each other's privacy

B – They think 'How nice' and invite them to dinner

C – The question doesn't apply, as they always go on group vacations with other Dutch people.

ANSWER = B

IF this ever happens, it's only on the 5th night of the seven days you're staying together at the same hotel.

TRUE ANSWER = A

When they're abroad, most Dutch people I've seen avoid each other like Superman and Kryptonite.

My wife and I were on a boat tour in the US once, and we heard another family speaking Dutch to each other. My wife was so concerned that they might hear her speaking to me with a Dutch accent that she adopted a British accent tor two hours. No matter what, she wanted to avoid getting into that conversation:

'*OH! Bent u ook Nederlandse!? Waar komen jullie vandaan? Wij komen uit Purmerend! Wat een leuke wolkenkrabbers, hoor!*'

Nederlanders gaan graag op vakantie
A – In Nederland
B – In Europa, bijvoorbeeld Frankrijk of Spanje
C – Overige.

Dutch people go on vacation mostly
A – In Nederland
B – In France or Spain
C – Elsewhere.

ANSWER = A

'We have Center Parcs for a reason!'

TRUE ANSWER = B

I've been on summer vacation in France, and the road is always choked with Dutch cars. We were standing still in traffic on the road by Orléans, and it was nothing but yellow license plates. You couldn't swing a dead cat without hitting a Dutch camper trailer, aka 'caravan,' aka *sleurhut*. I think of it as a national flooding drill. In case the dikes break, pack your 'snail house' and head south.

Maybe that's why Dutch people take everything when they go camping. We once saw a car that was too cool for a caravan; they'd just crammed everything into the back of their station wagon. The kids were playing their Nintendos with their faces pressed up against the windows. There was one poor girl with a sleeping bag on one side of her face, and a tent pole poking at her from above. And on the other side, there was something blue pressing up against her face, but we couldn't tell what it was. We pulled up a bit closer, and we saw it was a Senseo coffee machine, with the cylinder for the coffee pads, 'Because they may not have coffee in France.'

That's the way the Dutch go on holiday.

*

OPEN QUESTIONS

These questions I've added in – the issues they SHOULD put on the assimilation quiz.

The Netherlands is a country of bicycles. Biking etiquette is very important.

You are on a bike path, and you come across someone biking the wrong way. It someone you recognize. What do you do?
A – Wave but do not stop
B – Wave, stop and talk on the sidewalk
C – Politely criticize your friend for going the wrong way.

ANSWER = NONE OF THE ABOVE

Correct answer is:
Both stop in the middle of the path and chat for as long as possible while everybody crashes into each other trying not to hit you.

You are in a queue at a public event and someone sneaks to the front. What do you do?
A – Look the other way. Pointing only makes it worse
B – Politely point out that there is a line
C – Pretend like you know the person and also sneak to the front.

ANSWER = NONE OF THE ABOVE

Correct answer is:
Act like you've never heard of the concept of queuing and – if there are train doors involved – attempt to trample the slow and the weak.

*

The Netherlands is a country that values the right to privacy.

You are in public and someone is eating. What do you do?
A – Nod politely as you pass
B – Get something to eat yourself
C – Respect their privacy.

ANSWER = NONE OF THE ABOVE

Correct answer is:
Stare at them, point at them and say '*Eet smakelijk!*' as loudly as possible, as if to warn everyone in the area 'Watch out, this guy is eating in public and not at home or in a restaurant like normal people!'

Which of the following is NOT true?

A – Nederlanders are the most energetic in Europe

B – Nederlanders give the most to charity per capita in Europe

C – Nederlanders have the most positive attitude towards Muslims in Western Europe.

ANSWER = NONE OF THE ABOVE

They are all true, as reported by various news headlines.

How to Be Orange? *Wees trots, Oranje! Zo zie je er beter uit, echt!*

EPILOGUE

And if you Dutch people ever forget your influence on the rest of the world, just visit my parents' house in America. You can look around the room and point to the Dutch product names, headlines, and cultural icons that so many people take for granted:

Going around the room in any US apartment:

The TV. The light bulbs. The beer.
Not to mention ...
Tulips.
Pendulum clocks.
Orange-colored carrots ... AND:

The artwork hanging on your wall.
The long-life light bulb in your hall.

Dove or Axe, your household soap.
The invention of the microscope.

The first operational submarine.
The LED on your TV screen.

The ones who made the first CD.
DJs with the style 'hands-free.'

The pricey Shell Oil in your tank.
Likely some loans to your bank.

The ones who discovered New Zealand.
The inspiration for James Bond.

The fresh-cut flowers in your vase.
Kuipers, the bald guy up in space.

AkzoNobel and your car's color tone.
The ones who sang 'The Twilight Zone.'

Keeping New Orleans safe from the sea.
The Voice, that annoying show on TV.

Miffy the bunny, so cute you could eat.
And yes even Zwarte Piet.

Philips, Shell, KLM.
Unilever, Heineken.

Wesley Sneijder, Arjen Robben.
Anne Frank, Van Halen.

MC Escher, Hieronymus Bosch.
Rembrandt, Vincent van Gogh.

Erasmus, Spinoza, René Descartes.
Johan Cruyff. Barney and his darts.

Famke Janssen, Albert Heijn.
Carice van Houten, Anton Corbijn.

Bailing out Greece, Ireland, Spain.
Taking out the underwear bomber on your plane!

Being proud of values, some find strange.
That's How to be ORANGE.

ACKNOWLEDGMENTS

Inez de Goede, Bert van Essen, Erwin Lunstroo, Stephanie Dijkstra, Gerjan de Waard, Hayo Deinum, Boom Chicago, Pep Rosenfeld, Andrew Moskos, W. Shane Oman, DutchNews.nl, Robin Pascoe, Behind Dutch Headlines, Wytze van der Gaast, De Baak Institute, MC Theater, The British Language Training Centre, Eclipse AV, Peter de Goede, Sabine van Amft, Peter Grosz, David van Traa, Elena Lommers, Lesley Bevan, Andrea Dixon, Carol T. Tsaltas, Amy Abdou, Oscar van der Kroon, Jim Stolze, Simone Toppers, Carol Bontekoe, Stefan Kruger, David Schreurs, Jan Paternotte, Elvira van Hal. Politie Amsterdam-Amstelland. Special thanks to all the people too numerous to mention here.